DEDICATION
For Kelly, with love

1

Mom's worried voice came through the closed door. "Angie, are you all right?"

"Sure." The 14-year-old girl never took her eyes from the mirror. *Oh please, Mom, don't come into my room.*

"Are you sure?"

Angie squeezed her eyes shut. She ran one hand through her thick brown hair and sighed. *Give me a break, Mom. Just leave me alone.*

"I'm OK, Mom," she called. She waited, listening to Mom's quick steps clicking down the polished hall floor. For one wild moment she wanted to run after her, wanted to tell her everything. If only she could bury her face in Mom's lap the way she used to do before Dad died. The longing to get rid of her fear almost made her sick. She jerked her bedroom door open, then slowly closed it. She dared not tell Mom. She couldn't tell anyone. They'd all think she was crazy.

Maybe she was. Angie went back to her mirror. The small, pale girl looked scared but not crazy. She watched tears leak from the shadowy blue eyes and reached for a tissue. If she didn't hurry, she'd miss the bus. Frantically, she threw on her new jeans and T-shirt, grabbed a jacket, and clenched her teeth. But in those few moments she had reached a decision.

"I just won't make any more close friends. Then I won't be able to hurt them," she whispered to the girl who now watched from her bedroom mirror. Pain crept up her throat, and she wondered if she could toss off a bright smile to Mom as she fled through the back door. Yet the decision had brought a kind of numb relief. She hurried downstairs. "Don't have time for breakfast. 'Bye, Mom." Snatching the glass of milk from her place set at the breakfast table in the sunny corner, she downed it in one long gulp, ignored Mom's protest, and escaped.

Good. She'd gotten by Mom. Now she had time to put herself together before the bus came. In spite of herself, the familiar longing to run back to Mom almost undid all her good intentions. "Don't be stupid," she told herself fiercely. "High school students don't run home to mama every time they have a problem. Even a problem as real as mine—being a jinx."

Why had she said it out loud? Angie cringed and looked both ways. No one around yet, just the waving evergreens on both sides of the street where she lived. *Jinx.* The word hung in the clean September air. It seemed so real, now that she'd admitted it. She was glad when the bus came. It cut short her thoughts with the clamor of students. Angie smiled at some of the girls she'd met since she and Mom moved to Indian Creek, the small town near Portland, Oregon, but she didn't go sit with them. She took a seat by herself and stared out the window at the Columbia River. Today should be special—her first day as a freshman in the new four-year high school. Instead, she felt as if she were watching TV, seeing a girl named Angie Trescott registering for algebra, home ec, English I, PE, Oregon state history, and choir. Even lunch break was unreal.

By the time Angie got home from school, Mom had left for work. That was the one thing Angie hated about Indian Creek. She loved their simple cottage-style home, the roses and flowers and shrubs bright against the picket fence, and yellow painted house. She liked the feeling of security in the neighborhood. All of the neighbors worked in their yards and stopped to chat. All summer there'd been enough rain to wash the world but enough sun to cheer her up—and long evenings.

"I wish Mom didn't have to work—especially nights," Angie told their midnight-black cat, Mandrake. She felt dumb talking to a cat, but it was safer that way. She didn't think the jinx would rub off on a cat. Mandrake responded with a "Meowrr," and rubbed against her leg.

"OK, OK, so you're hungry." Angie couldn't help laughing. She dumped a small can of Seafood Surprise onto a paper plate and paused a moment to watch Mandrake daintily begin his supper. Finally she shrugged and took her lonely supper to the patio. Mount Hood gleamed with a fresh topping of snow, and Angie remembered that a neighbor had said he thought it would be an early winter. Some of Angie's loneliness dwindled. What snow they got in Los Angeles was rare and messy. It would be neat to actually get to play in snow!

She turned to her half-eaten meal. Her eyes stung. Mom always seemed to know when Angie was down and she wordlessly tried to cheer her with food. Tonight she'd left everything for taco salad and a big slice of chocolate cake, Angie's favorites. A tiny slip of white paper lay under a cup on her supper tray, just as always. Angie's lip curled down as she picked it up. "We are troubled on every side," it said, "yet not distressed; we are perplexed, but not in despair; persecuted, but not forsaken; cast down, but not destroyed."*

Angie didn't read the rest. If she dared, she'd tell Mom to stop leaving Scripture messages on the

---

* 2 Corinthians 4:8-9.

supper tray next to fresh flowers in a tiny vase. But she couldn't. It would hurt Mom too much. It would hurt her even more if she knew how angry Angie was with God.

Angie shoved the suddenly tasteless supper aside and glared at impersonal Mount Hood. "Just stand there. See if I care! You don't have to hurt and hurt and miss Dad." A torrent swept through her, breaking the dam of indifference she'd tried to build. Why had God let Dad die? She'd asked it a hundred times. Guilt replaced sorrow. It hadn't been Dad—it had been her.

"No!" Angie jumped up, flipping the tray over. Lettuce, beans, and corn chips flew. The little plastic vase clattered on the patio stone. Mandrake headed for the spilled food, but she didn't even see him. Hands clenched, she faced the giant mountain looming practically in her backyard. "I have to face it. Mom's gone for her eight-hour shift at the hospital. There's no one here to disturb me. Maybe if I can figure out when it all started, I can do something about it. But it's so hard remembering . . . " She swallowed hard. She closed her eyes and forced herself to relax, then dropped back into the padded patio chair. She bent down to pick up the pale pink rose. Its scent was light, delicate.

There had been roses back then, too. Angie had been almost 12. She and Dad and Mom lived near L.A., and Dad was a pilot. Angie loved both her parents, but Dad was special. He called her "Jinx" because funny little things happened when she was around.

"You look a little bit like Aunt Martha," he always teased. Angie had stared at the worn snapshot taken of an artist's sketch from long ago. Aunt Martha had lived in the colonies and had been accused of witchcraft. She had proved herself innocent against the unjust accusations.

"Am I a *witch*, Daddy?" Angie had asked anxiously. She felt cold all over.

"James!" Mom sounded a little cross. "You know there aren't any witches. Don't tease Angie."

"A jinx isn't a witch." Daddy smiled at Angie, and his eyes twinkled. Then when Angie couldn't keep a little worry from showing, he added, "You're my special good luck jinx. You can cast a spell on me any time."

Angie felt a little better after that—but deep down inside she always had a funny feeling when he called her Jinx. Because she loved him so much she never protested.

Then a few days before her twelfth birthday, the phone rang early in the morning. Angie had snuggled deeper under the covers, drifting and dreaming, until Mom came in the room. Her face was pale and tight. Her eyes were scared. She sat down on the bed and placed her hand on her daughter. Angie had closed her eyes. Suddenly she'd felt terribly frightened. "Angie." Mom's voice had sounded tiny.

"Uh-uh."

"Sit up, darling."

Angie wiggled upright. Mom hugged her fiercely and buried her face in her hair. When her voice came, it sounded cold and empty as though it came from the bottom of a deep, dark well.

"The phone call, Angie. There's been an accident."

Angie didn't reply, but her heart leaped into her throat.

Mom's voice was a mere whisper, the fluttering of butterfly wings against her daughter's hair. "A plane crash, honey."

Suddenly Angie couldn't breathe. "Daddy?"

"Daddy."

Mom held her, rocked her back and forth. But Angie twisted away. She shrugged off the covers and leaped out of bed. "I talked to him last night! He said he'd be home for dinner." Her eyes dared her mother to tell her different.

Mother's eyes were dark coals. She seemed to have trouble talking. "The telephone. That was someone from the airline. . . . At take-off. . . . the plane wouldn't climb. They won't know—"

"He called me Jinx!" Angie's voice squeaked in anger and disbelief. "Did I do it?"

"Of course not, Angie. It was an *accident*. You must never think you could have anything to do with it."

But long after Mom had gone out to call other family members, Angie lay staring at the ceiling. She tried to pray, but no words came. Finally she got up, dry-eyed, and put on the sky-blue dress Daddy had liked best. She knew it was all a mistake. Words didn't make it so. Daddy would be home for dinner. He'd promised. God wouldn't let him die.

It was no mistake. Investigation showed something had gone wrong with the airplane controls. When Angie heard that, she shivered. She remembered her father saying she could cast a spell on him any time. Maybe she had loved him too much.

Just maybe she was to blame. Weren't jinxes bad?

Somehow she lived through the funeral, the changes they had to make. It didn't take long to realize that Mom needed to work, to add to the insurance money Daddy had left for them. Mom was a registered nurse, and it was easy for her to start working again. They found a small apartment near the hospital so Mom could walk to work and yet be close if Angie needed her. But without Daddy, L.A. was no longer home. Mom began sending out letters, hunting a job closer to Portland, where some of her family lived. The result was an offer of night nurse at Indian Creek Hospital.

"I wish you weren't on nights," was all Angie let herself say. Mom mustn't know how terrified she was from the time it got dark until she heard Mom's key in the lock just after midnight. She never really slept until Mom came home. She wasn't particularly worried, just felt better once Mom had come. The shadows didn't seem scary if Mom was in the house.

Mom had never called Angie Jinx. Sometimes Angie wondered about it. Did Mom think . . . ? No. She didn't believe in such things. Gradually some of the guilt faded. Then Angie met 15-year-old Dave from across the street. The only teens on the block, they hit it off right away. All summer they played tennis and went swimming. There was nothing mushy. They just liked each other. Angie would be 15 the middle of September, so there wasn't too much difference in their ages.

"You'll love Indian Creek High School," Dave bragged one afternoon. "And wait until you see some of our games!" He leaped in an imaginary jump shot. "Our Braves are the best basketball team in the tournament."

"And I suppose you're the star forward," Angie teased.

"Nope. Just scrub team. But I'm going to be star forward when I'm a junior and senior."

He sounded so positive that she was surprised. "How come?"

"Well, God gave me a talent for playing basketball, and it's my responsibility to be the best I can."

Angie couldn't believe her ears. "David Jackson! What a thing to say!"

He quirked his sandy eyebrows at her and grinned. His freckles looked dark against his tan skin and white teeth. "The way I figure it is that guy in the Bible that had 10 talents, well, they weren't *all* big, were they? Chances are, some were big and some little. So I have a talent for sports. I'm not about to bury it in a hole like that other guy who had one talent. Remember what happened to him! God said he was wicked and a rotten servant."

"I don't think the Bible reads quite like that!" Angie protested.

Dave grinned again. "Close enough."

"I-I wish I was close to God like that." Angie didn't quite keep the tremble from her voice. "I used to be. Before Dad died." She clamped her lips shut. A wave of red came into her face. She could feel it burning.

David didn't ask questions. But for the very first time he leaned over and gave her a hug. "You're OK, Angie. Just give God a chance." Before she could move he ran lightly down her front steps.

"Gotta go. See you tonight at our youth meeting."

"Not if I see you first," Angie managed to taunt, although she couldn't help grinning.

"Don't be witchy," he tossed the words over his shoulder.

Instantly Angie's warmth disappeared. She opened her mouth to shriek at him. Her face whitened, her fingernails bit into the palms of her hands. *Witchy.* A terrible feeling rose to her throat, the same as when she knew Dad had been killed. *Something was going to happen to Dave.* She had to warn him. But how? He was out the gate and halfway across the street by now.

What would she have said, anyway? "Don't like me too much. Don't be my friend. I'm a jinx. I hurt people, maybe even killed my own father." Even in her mind it sounded like a soap opera, not anything a Christian boy would believe.

Her hands unclenched. Sweat beads stood on her forehead. "You are being absolutely insane," she told herself. "You have no control over others. It's just because he happened to pick that one word." But a little voice inside whispered, "Why did he choose *that* word?"

Angie spent the rest of the evening sitting on the patio. She left a note on the front door that she didn't feel well and wouldn't be going to the youth meeting. She heard Dave come, then leave—and she felt more miserable than ever. Mingled with her misery was the same heavy feeling she hadn't been able to get rid of even by watching TV, or listening to the stereo, or even blindly trying to read the Bible.

"Why, Angie! You still up?" Angie looked up to

see Mom standing in the doorway. Angie automatically noted how trim Mom looked in her white pantsuit. Her blue eyes and brown hair, so like what Angie saw in her mirror every day, didn't hide shadows of weariness. She must have had a bad shift.

"You needn't have worried about Dave, you know." Mom hung her windbreaker in the closet, missing Angie's muffled gasp of horror. "He's going to be just fine. His arm will heal long before basketball season, and—"

Angie didn't hear the rest. She could feel the blood drain from her face, leaving her a little dizzy. "Mom?" she could barely get it out. *"What happened?"*

2

What happened?" Angie repeated.

Mom's eyes reflected amazement. "I thought you knew. Dave was brought in to the hospital a few hours ago. It was the funniest thing. He said he couldn't remember exactly what happened. He was on his way home from our place when all of a sudden he was lying on the sidewalk with his arm hanging at a strange angle and hurting like crazy. He thinks he must have tripped on a rough piece of concrete. He's embarrassed and disgusted about the whole thing."

Mom's eyes twinkled. "Guess he feels like a klutz—not a good image for a supposed-to-be-graceful ballplayer!" She dropped to a chair and kicked off her shoes. "I wouldn't talk too much about it when I see him if I were you. He's staying overnight at the hospital but will be home tomorrow."

"No, I won't talk about it too much."

Mom must have missed the dangerously quiet note in Angie's voice. Within a few moments they were both in bed but sleep eluded Angie.

So it was true. She really was a jinx in spite of what Mom said. It must be because she cared too much about people—like she'd been starting to really care about Dave. But what could she do about it?

Angie tossed and turned, finally falling into a restless sleep where a voice called, "Jinx! It's all right," then faded before she could decide who was calling. She got up, ate a bowl of cereal, then haunted the window that opened to the Jackson yard. Finally she walked around outside. She sat down on a side step, head in her hands. The next thing she knew she saw Dave climbing out of their station wagon, hollering at her. "Hey, come cheer up an invalid," he called.

Angie looked up. "You don't look like an invalid

except for the cast," she pointed out.

"Not long for this world, Angie!" He faked a hollow cough. "What's wrong? I'm just goofing off. Hey, don't cry. I'm OK."

"Sorry," she sniffled. For one wild moment she considered dumping it all out. Maybe his strong faith in God could help her. "Dave, I—"

He couldn't have heard her mumble. "Angie, I've got some bad news," he said as they walked toward his porch.

Was his arm going to be crooked or paralyzed or something? Angie's heart skipped a beat, and she held her breath.

"We're going away."

Relief warred with disappointment. "Going away! Where, and why?"

"Dad's being assigned to Boeing in Seattle for a special project. He thinks it's only for a year, so we'll lease the house." Dave's gaze was steady. "Seattle isn't so far away that I can't see you sometimes, but it means not being together like we have this summer . . ." His voice trailed off, and he looked away.

Angie breathed again. Now she wouldn't have to tell. Dave would be far enough from her so she couldn't hurt him.

"I didn't know until Mom told me this morning. Orders just came through. We're leaving in a few weeks."

"It's OK." But Angie's words were flat. It was better this way. If he'd stayed, she would have had to tell him she wasn't going to see him anymore. Now she didn't have to do that, either. Good! She hugged her secret to herself. He'd probably write a few letters, and she might even answer; then they'd both stop writing. The same way she'd done with her Los Angeles friends. She wouldn't let him know how much she'd miss him. When he moved back they'd be a lot more grown-up and have other circles of friends. The broken arm might just be a warning. She wouldn't take any chances with things getting worse if she stayed his friend. But inside she felt that she was bleeding. The question came over and over, *Why do I have to be a jinx?*

The two weeks stretched out, and it was actually almost September before Dave and his family moved. Angie defied her growing hopelessness and still played tennis and swam with Dave. Surely nothing would happen now that he was moving. Besides, she made sure they were always busy or around others. Sometimes she caught Dave watching her in a funny way, but she didn't care. She was protecting him in the only way she knew how.

Then he was gone. "I'll write," he promised.

"Good." She laughed nervously. "Have a super year, and don't forget to tell me all about basketball and stuff." She kept up the bright talk until Mom called her to dinner and never gave Dave a chance for a goodbye kiss. But after picking at the food, she headed for bed and cried herself to sleep.

Had it only been last night? Angie came back to the present. The sun was down now and the evening turning cold, but no colder than her heart. How would it be to go through freshman year without any friends? Or maybe for the rest of her life? A new thought struck her. What about Mom? Was she in danger too?

"No, oh, no . . . " but once planted, the thought

took root and grew faster than Jack's beanstalk. Mom was the only thing left in Angie's life that really mattered. With Dave gone and God so far away, Mom meant everything in the world. What if something happened to her? Angie shuddered, turned off the patio light, and stood under a hot shower for a long, long time, trying to drive the cold chill of fear from her body.

It didn't work. She awakened in the night and crept to the open doorway of Mom's bedroom time after time, just listening to Mom breathe and thanking God that everything was all right.

Then she retreated into herself. If Mom wanted to do something special, Angie always had to study. She knew she was hurting Mom, but wasn't it better for Mom to be disappointed than for her to be—she never finished the sentence. Mom was so little, so vulnerable.

But Connie Gregory wasn't vulnerable. Neither could she be discouraged. She and her aunt moved into Dave's house the week after the Jacksons left. And just a few days before Angie's fifteenth birthday, tall, blonde Connie raced for the bus stop and screeched to a halt. "Hi, Angie. I know all about you, and I like what I hear. Wanta be my Jeff?" At Angie's blank stare she laughed. "You know—like the cartoon characters, Mutt and Jeff. I always have best friends who are shorter than me. Oh, my aunt Ida works with your mom."

Some of the chains around Angie's heart loosened. She'd been so lonely since Dave moved. Even though it was her own fault, it was hard to walk alone. Connie was tall and strong, too strong to be hurt. What if she and Connie became friends—

Mutt and Jeff, as Connie had said? It didn't seem possible anyone that strong could be affected even by a jinx.

Angie took a deep breath and blew a stray curl out of her eyes. "I'd love to be your Jeff," she said defiantly. She had cut the ties holding her to the past. Not only was Connie Gregory going to be her friend, Connie was going to be the means by which Angie left all this jinx stuff behind. For Angie had seen a tiny Testament in Connie's bag.

"My guide," Connie had explained. "I always carry it."

A tall, strong girl who carried a Bible as a guide! Maybe through Connie and her Bible, Angie could increase her own faith and finally be free.

In the days before her birthday, Angie watched to see if she was doing anything that might hurt her new friend. Sometimes she couldn't help being moody, but Connie wasn't about to let her get away with it. She always had something bubbly to say. Yet she stood up for what she believed, in class and everywhere else. She also took Indian Creek by storm and carried Angie right along with her. Angie overheard one girl say, "If I thought I could be as instantly popular as Connie Gregory, *I'd* start carrying a Bible too!"

So when Connie hollered up the stairs on Sunday night, Angie's birthday, half the kids in the freshman class were right there yelling, "Happy birthday, Angie!"

"You didn't tell me," Angie accused, but she was thrilled. It was the first surprise party she'd ever had. Dad and Mom used to take her out to dinner and once had some girls over, but she'd never had a party like the swarm of laughing kids spread out in the living room now.

"Anything for a party." Connie's eyes were filled with mischief. "Even Jeff's birthday!" Connie knew a bunch of neat things to do from kid games like breaking balloons on wrists and ankles to keeping a straight face during jokes. Connie had cleared the surprise with Angie's mom. Mom had gotten off work and kept pizza and cake coming until it looked like a buffet.

"Connie's the best thing that's happened to me in ages," Angie told Mom as they were cleaning up after the party.

"I heard that." Connie appeared in the doorway. She'd run home and changed into old jeans. "The nicest thing about me is my willingness to help clean up." She grabbed a stack of mangled, stained paper plates. "Ugh, was that ever food?"

"You know," Angie stopped in the process of loading the dishwasher, "I've always hated it when people laughed at me, but tonight I didn't mind."

"That's 'cause no one was laughing *at* you. They were all laughing *with* you," Connie said.

"How come you're so smart about all that stuff?" Mom had gone into the dining room with the silver, and the girls were alone.

"Being an Army brat, moving all over." For the first time Angie saw the depths of Connie's feelings. "Just when I started making friends we'd move on. I learned I had to take happiness with me. That's when I began carrying my Bible." Her dark-blue eyes deepened even more. "I've been so happy even the few weeks I've been here, knowing that at least for a year I get to stay in one school. Dad and

Mom are in Africa and decided I'd be better off remaining in the States, so good old Aunt Ida gave up her one-bedroom apartment. My folks know the Jacksons and leased the house for us. Angie," she leaned close, "you can't imagine what it's like to feel roots after years of being shuttled back and forth between continents."

"I never knew you had any problems," Angie blurted out.

"Who doesn't?" Connie's mood changed. "I just don't intend to let them get me down. I miss my parents a lot, but I know they're OK." She grinned. "By the way, Dave Jackson's kinda cute, isn't he? I used to have a crush on him when I was a kid."

"Oh?" Angie's heart sank. If Connie ever liked Dave, there was no chance for her, even if she weren't a jinx and hadn't closed the door between them, which she had.

"Yeah, 'way back when I was 13."

"Poor old lady!" Angie stood on tiptoe and pretended to examine Connie's long blonde hair. "I don't see any gray yet, but before long—"

"Enough, enough." Connie tossed the tea towel to the sink. "I guess we're through for tonight," she said with a yawn. "See you tomorrow."

She turned to go, then stopped. "Angie, I have something really special to suggest. Something we can do together. But first," she hesitated, "do you think you might like to be a nurse someday?"

"A nurse!" Angie thought of Mom working different shifts and putting in hard hours. "I don't think so."

"Think of all the hurting people you could help."

Think of all the hurting people I could hurt worse! The words trembled on Angie's lips, but she bit them back.

Connie seemed to forget that she had to get home. She dropped to the kitchen table and parked her feet on a utility chair. Her eyes were enormous. "Ever since I was a little kid I've known I wanted to be a nurse. Now that I live with Aunt Ida and have had a chance to see what she and your mom do, the feeling is stronger than ever. I just thought maybe if you felt the same way, we could start getting ready by taking lots of science—which I hate."

Angie's thoughts were in a whirl. She chose her words carefully. "I just can't be a nurse," she said slowly.

"At least think about it." Connie slid easily off the table. "Think about all the fun we could have rooming together and helping each other in training. Don't get obnoxious about it, but you're the only person I've ever liked well enough to ask to consider planning ahead that far."

Angie's mouth fell open. "But—"

"See ya." And Connie was gone.

"Funny," Angie said to Mom as they were getting ready for bed, "Connie said she had something really neat to suggest, then she didn't tell me what it was."

"You can always ask her tomorrow," Mom said. Angie shrugged. She wished she'd thought to ask before Connie left. Or maybe Connie had decided not to tell. Maybe she was disappointed that Angie didn't want to be a nurse.

Maybe it wasn't such a bad idea after all. At

least if she blew it, people would be right there to patch up her victims! Angie chuckled over her own morbid thought and opened her bedroom window a crack. She could see across the yard that Connie's bedroom was dark. No last minute wave tonight. Somehow it seemed significant. Pushing down a nagging little worry, Angie forced herself to relax. Connie was too good a friend to let a difference of opinion over future careers separate them.

Angie struggled from the depths of sleep when the phone rang. Mom must be beat. She wasn't answering as she normally did. Angie padded to the phone and glanced at her watch at the same time. "Hello?"

"Angie, this is Ida Gregory. I hate to call this time of night, but Connie's sick, and I'm taking her to the hospital. Could you ask your mother to come over, please?" Aunt Ida hung up.

The receiver slipped from Angie's fingers. She caught it just before it clanked to the floor. Terror filled her. *Give me a break, Lord,* her heart cried.

It had started again. As soon as Connie let her know how much she cared.

3

For one dreadful moment Angie thought she was going to be sick. Clenching her fists until the nails bit into her palms, she raced for Mom's bed-room, yanked open the door, and pelted through. "Mom, wake up!"

Aren't you glad this happened during a night when Mom wasn't working? part of her mind whispered. She ignored the little voice and shook her mother. "Mom, wake up!"

Her mother sat up, eyes fogged, but brain alert, the trained nurse responding to a need. "What's wrong, Angie?"

"It's Connie. She's really sick, and she'll probably need to go to the hospital. Mrs. Gregory wants you to come over."

Her mother was already out of bed, snatching a robe, sliding her feet into slippers. "Did she say anything specific about how Connie was acting?" Mom reached for the bag she always kept packed. It wasn't the first time she'd been called to neighborhood duty since they came to Indian Creek. She never minded. "It's a skill I've been given," she had told Angie. "I'm just glad I can use it. Besides, it's a witness of Christ's love. You'd be surprised how often I'm able to get in a word or two for Him when I go on my 'unofficial duty' calls."

Angie swallowed a lump in her throat and answered Mom's question. "She didn't say anything except that Connie was terribly sick." She turned her face away so Mom wouldn't see her cry. She was too old to be blubbering like a frightened child.

Once Mom left the house, Angie sprang into action. She slid a pair of jeans over her PJs, huddled into the brand-new ski jacket that had been her birthday present from Mom, and slipped out the door. Without attracting attention, she got across the yard and hid next to the front door, screening herself behind a spruce tree.

"I have to see her for myself," Angie whispered to a night that had changed from party weather to threatening. It was pitch black except for light streaming from the house. Not a star overhead—just great boiling black masses. It was going to storm. But the storm outside had nothing on the storm inside Angie.

She didn't have long to wait. Moments later, Angie saw Mom and Mrs. Gregory half carrying Connie to the car. They helped her lie down on the back seat. Mom tucked a blanket around her even as Mrs. Gregory slid behind the wheel.

"Now drive carefully," Mom said. "The hospital is only a couple of miles away.

"I'll close up the house," she called as the car backed out of the driveway. "God bless!" Mom watched until the car turned a corner; then she went back into the house.

At that, Angie raced back home. She was out of her jeans and into a warm, comforting robe when Mom returned. "What's wrong with Connie?" she burst out.

Mom shook her head. "We won't know for sure until she gets to the hospital. It could be several things. She's having bad abdominal pain, and she's nauseated and sweaty. Both Ida and I suspect appendicitis."

"Is it my fault?" The question came without her thinking. Angie wished she'd kept still.

Mom's blue eyes opened wide. "What on earth are you talking about? How could it be *your* fault?"

Angie retreated into herself when more than anything she wanted to run to Mom and throw herself into her arms. "It's just that she worked so hard on my party and everything . . . " Her voice trailed off. The words sounded lame even to her.

"Nonsense. Your party had nothing to do with it if it's appendicitis." Mom's face relaxed into a grin. "Of course, if it turns out she ate too much junk food . . ." She yawned. "Sorry, honey, I've got to get back to bed. So do you." She came close, put her arms around Angie, and drew her close. "Connie will be fine. That's why we have doctors and nurses and hospitals."

Not fully convinced but desperately wanting to be, Angie said, "Goodnight—no, good morning, Mom, and thanks." She turned away so Mom wouldn't see the way her chin trembled. But sleep wouldn't come. How could Connie have become so sick so soon? A few hours before she'd been laughing and clowning around. How could she get so sick so fast? Angie shivered and cried herself back to sleep after a tangled prayer for God to take care of her friend.

When the phone rang again, she felt herself struggle through layers of time, trying to get her eyes open. She heard Mom's crisp voice. "Yes? Oh, good. Yes, I'll tell her."

Angie let out the breath she'd been holding. Mom wouldn't sound like that if it weren't good news.

"Angie?" Mom's smiling face peeked around the door. "Connie is minus one appendix and doing great."

Relief flooded through Angie. Joy exploded like an Independence Day skyrocket. "Thank God!"

Mom's eyes softened. "Yes, indeed. She evidently had one red-hot appendix. It burst in the container after they'd removed it."

Some of Angie's joy dimmed. "Then, if they hadn't taken it when they did—"

"They did take it, Angie." Mom sat on the edge of the bed and turned back the coverlet. "With the new drugs, even a burst appendix and its results can usually be controlled, but getting it out intact is always the best way. It keeps infection from spreading through a person's system." She smiled her special crinkly smile at Angie. "Well, as long as I'm up, how would you like pancakes for breakfast?"

Angie's churning stomach revolted at the thought. "Thanks, Mom, but toast and juice are fine." She rolled over and away from the funny expression on Mom's face, slid from bed, and started for the bathroom.

"Angie, is something wrong?" Sympathy lines creased Mom's usually unlined face.

Angie whirled toward Mom. "Wha-what do you mean?"

Mom's steady eyes never left Angie's face. "I mean you are acting so strange about this whole thing blaming yourself." She ran a tired hand across her uncombed hair.

Again Angie longed to share her burden. She opened her mouth. Slowly closed it. Mom would think she was crazy if she said she simply couldn't get over feeling she brought bad luck to her friends! She hastily substituted, "Guess I didn't get enough sleep. A shower will make a new woman out of me." She deliberately smiled and was rewarded with seeing Mom's face relax. In a final attempt to reassure her mother, she added, "On second thought, maybe I will take those pancakes." The perk of Mom's eyebrows almost made it worthwhile.

The breakfast table was cheery. Even though rumbling clouds chased each other outside the multipaned dining room window, Mom had made the inside pretty. A small yellow chrysanthemum plant sat on a blue tablecloth, along with glasses of bright orange juice. Angie found she was able to eat after all. The first few bites were the hardest, and after that she managed fine.

"May I go see Connie after school?" she wanted to know.

Mom hesitated, and a pucker creased her forehead. "I'm not sure. It might be better to wait a day or two until she's stronger."

The last half of Angie's pancake tasted like sawdust. Why would Connie need to be stronger before seeing her best friend? Sudden suspicion stopped a final forkful halfway to her mouth. Had Mom suspected Angie might be . . . ? No, it wasn't possible. She carefully placed her fork across her plate. *Jinx. Angie's a jinx.*

"Gotta finish getting ready." She jumped up, planted a quick kiss on top of Mom's head, and escaped. Once in her own room, she mechanically brushed her hair, reached for her books, and started out.

It was one of the worst days of her entire life. Bombarded with questions, she felt herself congealing. Why did everyone have to talk about Connie? "No, I haven't seen her yet." "Yes, Aunt Ida says she's fine." "Not sure when she can come home." "Yes, it was really sudden, wasn't it? No warning at all." From the time she caught the bus until the glad instant she stepped down from it, feeling let out of prison, Angie kept up her guard. She barely managed to return the "See you tomorrow" farewells and stumble up the path to the quiet, deserted home, glad for the first time Mom wasn't there to meet her.

"This has got to stop," she ordered herself after she'd collapsed to the couch. "All these things are just happenings. There's no way I could have had anything to do with them." She took a deep breath. "God, You have seemed kind of far away since Dad died. Please—" She didn't even know exactly what to pray for, so she sighed and gave up. Mandrake meowed, and she carried him to the kitchen and fed him, glad for his cheerful purr.

After a sketchy supper Angie settled to her books. One good thing, she'd learned that her own problems dwindled when she concentrated on getting her lessons done. She was amazed when the phone rang, and she glanced at the ticking wall clock. Eight-thirty. "Hello?"

"Good news, Angie." Mom's bright voice filled the room. "You can come see Connie after school tomorrow, and she'll probably be home the day after." Mom's voice rattled on. ". . . doing fine . . . anxious to see you . . . must dash . . . lunch break almost over . . ."

The hours seemed endless the next day, and for the first time Angie stumbled over answers during discussion in her classes. Morning clouds had given way to brilliant, dancing sunshine and a little breeze that whisked yellow leaves into her path. It wasn't a long walk from school to the low hospital building. Hardly took half an hour. One good thing about Indian Creek, it was small enough so everything important was within a fairly easy walking distance. At first Angie practically ran. But as she neared her destination her steps slowed and her breath quickened. The hospital lay in the mellow September sun, peaceful, reassuring. Yet she knew that inside people were sick and struggling.

"Kind of like me," she acknowledged, eyes fixed on a clambering vine by a window. "Peaceful enough outside but not like that inside." She pushed the morbid thought away and slowly opened the front door.

"Hi, Angie."

She spun around, a big smile growing. Mom!

"I knew you'd be getting here just about now." Mom looked professional in her white pantsuit. She linked her arm in Angie's and led her down a long hall. Angie looked around curiously. She hadn't been in a hospital since she was seven and had her tonsils out. Her memories of then included white walls and finding it hard to swallow. What a difference here! The walls of Indian Creek Hospital were painted soft green with white trim. Here and there murals of the Oregon coast, Mount Hood, and the like brightened the hallway.

"Why, it's great!"

"I've been telling you you should pay us a visit here," Mom reminded, eyes proud. "And the service and care are even better than the decor." She swung a door inward to a small, two-bed sunny room. The bed closest to the door was empty, but in the window bed a familiar figure lay propped against pillows, eager eyes on the doorway.

"Hi, Connie." Angie crossed the room, fingers clenching and unclenching. Connie didn't look sick at all! A little pale, maybe, but certainly not the way she'd looked such a short time before.

"About time they let you in," Connie grumbled, then grinned at Angie. "I wanted you here as soon as I came out from under the anesthetic!" Her dark-blue eyes sparkled. "What's the use of creating one big stir if your best friend can't be with you?"

Angie's knees buckled and she dropped into a visitor's chair.

"Not too long, Angie," Mom warned. Angie could see her ineffectually trying to smother a smile. She waved and went out, leaving the door open behind her.

"So what's with school? Did anybody miss me?" Connie wanted to know.

The blessed letdown of seeing her friend so almost back to normal loosened Angie's tongue. "Miss you! Would you miss Mutt if you saw a cartoon strip with just Jeff in it?" She slowly let tension drain out of her fingers. "You'd have thought yourself pretty important if you could have heard the kids. They acted as if you'd died or something." Angie caught her breath. She could feel her face turning ashen. Why had she said such a terrible thing?

Connie didn't seem to notice. "More than one way to get attention," she said with a giggle. Then, "Just kidding. I was pretty sick. I'm just glad God saw to it I got here when I did." She turned solemn eyes on Angie. "When I first woke up, I wasn't going to bother Aunt Ida. Then things got pretty scary and I thought I was going to pass out, so I hollered."

"I'm glad you did."

"Me too." Connie dropped the serious tone, and Angie was glad. "One good thing. I know now I will be a nurse someday. Before, it was sort of a dream, but after seeing what the nurses do, the way that even when you're scared and sick, they talk you out of it, that's for me." She wiggled and adjusted her pillows. "Have you thought about it?"

"No," Angie confessed. "If certain people insist on staging fright scenes in the middle of the night, those people can't expect others to concentrate on the future."

"Nut!" Connie laughed, and Angie joined her. It was good to laugh. It might also detract from Connie's discussing nursing.

It didn't. Connie persisted, eyes glowing. "You just can't imagine how neat it is watching the nurses. My doctor's swell, and if it didn't take forever, I might be a doctor."

Angie shuddered. "Ugh! I can't think of any-thing worse."

"I said *might*. I'm not going to be, anyway. I don't want to give up that many years to prepar-ing." Connie's eyes flashed. "Besides, doctors are always getting called in the middle of the night by people like me! Nurses are too, but not as much." She leaned forward, made a face. "My incision's still sore."

Fascinated, Angie listened as Connie rushed on. "You know at the party when I said I had something to tell you? Something neat?"

"Uh-huh. I wondered afterward why you didn't."

"Got busy talking about other stuff." Connie's cheeks had turned bright red. "I've just been busting to get you here so I could tell you how we can really be of service."

"Sorry, Angie, time's up." Mom's capped head poked around the corner.

"Oh, Mrs. Trescott, I have something special to tell Angie!" Connie wailed.

Mom was firm. "Sorry, Connie, it'll have to keep." She laid a practiced hand on Connie's wrist. "Your pulse is a little fast and your face is on fire. So much excitement isn't good for you. Out, Angie." Her understanding grin took the sting from the order.

"Come see me tomorrow when I get home," Connie pleaded. "My news will have to keep."

Angie smiled and slipped out, leaving Mom chatting with Connie. Looked as though she'd have to wait again to hear Connie's terrific suggestion. The sun had dropped while she was inside. Should she call a cab or walk? She watched the golden glow over the town she was learning to love and call home. Two miles. She'd walk. She could just about make it before it got dark, and there were no dangerous or deserted areas for her to pass. Just well-kept homes, the school, small business district.

"I couldn't have walked like this if we'd stayed in a big city," she told her complaining cat when she reached home. Mandrake sniffed indignantly. "OK, I know your supper's late." She fed and petted him, then watched the last rays of twilight from the patio. The half-formed plans to stay away from Connie as much as she could without seeming unfriendly melted. Uneasy peace settled over her. Connie was going to be fine. She hadn't been jinxed at all.

"All right!" She stretched, smiled, and felt a load slide from her shoulders. With a final glance at the horizon, Angie stepped inside and locked the patio door. She had an algebra test in the morning and needed to review.

"Wonder what Connie is up to now?" she asked Mandrake. His rumbled answer was unintelligible, and with a pat of his soft fur she settled down to the wonderful world of formulas.

4

Connie and I had quite a chat last night," Mom told Angie at breakfast the next morning. "She couldn't seem to get sleepy, and she admitted she didn't feel as well as she had."

Angie nearly choked

on a bite of toast. Had her visit upset Connie? Oh, no! "She wasn't worse, was she?"

"Of course not." Mom's smile seemed like a ray of sunlight piercing Angie's fear. "It's typical for patients to get a bit feverish at night."

Angie barely heard her. She could feel the cold chunk of lead that must be her heart clunking in her throat. She bit her lower lip. Was the only way to protect Connie to just keep away from her? Her spirits dropped at the thought. No more Mutt and Jeff? Might as well take the basket out of basket-ball.

She caught Mom's speculative gaze on her and roused. "So what did you talk about?"

"You."

"Me!" Her heart leaped. Did they—?

Mom pushed her chair back. The blue cotton blouse she'd donned for housework brought out the color of her eyes. "Remember when you said Connie was the best thing that had happened to you since you came to Indian River?"

Angie nodded, not trusting herself to speak.

"It seems she feels the same about you." Mom's expression turned pixie. "Now don't go getting conceited, but you're one special person to your friend Connie." She rose and began gathering dishes.

A warm glow began to melt some of the ice inside Angie. "I'm glad she feels that way."

The glow lasted all day at school. It didn't bother Angie that the kids yelled down the halls asking about Connie. She could proudly pass on that Connie was OK and would be home that afternoon.

"Has she come?" Angie burst breathlessly in on Aunt Ida after the school bus dropped her.

"Not yet." The gray-haired woman with the wide smile welcomed her. "Come on in. I just baked cookies, the ones Connie likes best." She led Angie to the sweet-smelling kitchen and put a plate of warm sugar cookies in front of her.

"Mmm, good." Angie loved the extra vanilla taste. "When's Connie coming?"

"They decided to keep her one more day," Aunt Ida told her.

Angie's fingers, reaching for another cookie, froze in midair. "Why?"

"The doctor got called out on an emergency and wasn't able to get in and sign her release." Aunt Ida looked up in surprise. "It's just a formality. Connie's fine."

"Good!" Angie mechanically took another cookie and bit into it. Why did she have to jump like a startled bird every time some little thing didn't go as she expected?

Aunt Ida leaned forward, gray eyes serious behind her glasses. "You know, Angie, you'll never know what you've done for Connie."

Angie could hear the steady *tick-tock, tick-tock* of the wall clock as she stared at Aunt Ida. "What I've done for her?"

"That's right. I've wanted to thank you for the longest time, but," a flash of expression made her look like her niece for a moment, "it seems Mutt and Jeff are never very far apart! I've not had a chance to see you alone."

Angie couldn't say a word. She glanced around the cheerful old-fashioned kitchen then back at

Aunt Ida, who fit her environment so well.

"For a long time Connie has wanted to stay in one place instead of being shuttled from area to area. When her parents discovered they were going to be sent to Africa, it seemed the time." Light glinted in Aunt Ida's glasses. "I'd been wanting to have her come for years! Anyway, she was excited about it, but she wasn't sure if she could stay away from her parents that long. The other thing"—her fingers drummed on the spotless tabletop—"is that the part of Africa they are in is a potential danger spot. There's no telling if the unrest could break out into something worse."

Angie's eyes opened wide. All this time Connie had been worried about her parents and never said anything? She'd never even guessed, in spite of all the sharing they'd done.

Aunt Ida poured milk in their glasses. "We arranged it that if Connie absolutely couldn't stand being away, I'd ship her to Africa, although that wasn't a good solution either. But the very first day of school she came bouncing in . . . "

Angie could almost see how it happened: Connie's long, blonde hair glistening in the sun, deep blue eyes with little lights flickering in them.

"I'd told her a lot about you, and she could hardly wait to get here and meet you. When she got home she told me, 'Angie's all you said and more.' You should have seen her dancing around the living room. 'I've found my Jeff,' she said, 'and what a year it's going to be!'"

Angie's throat hurt. She'd known Connie liked her, but not like this!

Aunt Ida wasn't finished. "When she was planning your party, she told me just watching you come home to an empty house made her realize how lucky she was. Her folks plan to take early retirement at the end of this year; she was a 'later in life' baby. She noticed that you and your mother don't get to spend a lot of time together. 'One year, then my folks will be home for keeps,' she said. 'I'm so thankful.'"

The oven timer bell rang sharply and Aunt Ida removed another pan of cookies, then came back to the table where Angie sat, mind turning. "You two have the special kind of friendship that can last a lifetime. You will have many friends, but just one or two that will still be as close to you when you're both 40 or 60, no matter how far apart you are. Such a friendship is a real blessing, Angie. I hope nothing ever comes between you and Connie."

"I won't let it," Angie promised fiercely, ignoring the reminding thump of her heart that seemed to mock her. She slid from her chair. "Thanks for the cookies and the talk." She smiled at Aunt Ida and hurried out the door.

All evening bits and pieces of what Aunt Ida had told her danced on the pages of her school books, shimmered in the air. Never had Angie felt so humble. To think a popular, beautiful girl like Connie thought that much of her! It was hard to believe, yet Aunt Ida had been positive. Angie tossed her pencil to the desk and clasped her hands behind her head. Maybe it was because they were both only children. Connie was just like the sister she'd always secretly longed for—no, better. Most of the sisters she knew argued a lot, and she and Connie had never even disagreed yet.

"Yet!" She repeated the word aloud and wandered to the patio door. It had grown dark, and there were no stars or moon in sight. Why did a strange feeling go over her?

"You're getting paranoid," she told herself disgustedly and forced her attention back to her books.

Less than 24 hours later Angie and Connie held their grand reunion. "You'd think we've been apart forever instead of just a few days," Connie chuckled. She lay on the couch surrounded by a couple pots of flowers, cards, and the usual home-from-the-hospital clutter.

"It seemed forever," Angie sighed. It had. Maybe because today at school she'd even wondered if Connie would come home after all. "You're looking good."

"Naturally." Connie stretched her mouth in a big smile, then stretched her arms out. "Boy, home is one great place to be. Hospitals are OK for sick people, but I'm glad to be out of there. Wasn't your party a smash? I haven't had as much fun in years. Remember how Sarah and Ken looked when their balloons broke?"

"Do I! I never knew anyone could get so competitive over a silly party game." Angie let a little smile tease her lips. It was good to have Connie her old self.

"Takes all kinds, I guess." Connie sat up straight. "Know what we're going to do when I get back to school?"

"I have a feeling I'm going to find out," Angie teased.

Connie successfully ignored the interruption. "We're going to be Teen Aides."

"What on earth is that? Something like a Band-Aid?"

Connie threw a colorful pillow at her. "No, dummy. It's what Indian River Hospital calls their nurses' aides. I found out all about it when I was there. I'd been thinking about it earlier. That's what I was going to tell you." She stopped for breath, then went on, "We're both 15, so we qualify. Even mature 14-year-olds sometimes get to be Teen Aides, but girls who may want to be nurses can have a chance to see what it's like." She sat back, a cat-ate-the-goldfish grin all over her face.

Angie felt as if someone had cut the ground out from under her, leaving her to fall through space. "Hey, wait a minute! I promised to think about being a nurse, not to be some junior angel of mercy."

"Don't you *want* to do it?" Connie asked, a hurt look coming into her eyes. "I think it will be absolutely great! We'll see your mom and Aunt Ida sometimes, and . . . "

Angie tuned her out. She could feel herself being torn two ways. Her old fears surfaced. *If she was still a jinx, she might*—she shivered. But Aunt Ida had said never to let anything come between them, and she had promised nothing ever would. She could see how much this meant to Connie. If she refused, would it make a rift between them?

"You aren't even listening, Angie Trescott," Connie accused. "You act like my big news is absolutely nothing." All her excitement fled, and her mouth drooped.

"I want to do it, but I can't." Angie shoved one hand over her mouth, but too late.

Connie pounced on it. "Why not?"

"I can't tell you." Angie saw that made things worse. "Trust me, will you? A hospital is no place for me, even as a Teen Aide." Her voice shook, and she ducked her head so Connie couldn't see the expression on her face.

It seemed hours before Connie finally said, "You might as well tell me the whole thing. Something's eating on you, isn't it? Several times I've caught you acting strange, like when you said people at school were as curious as if I'd died. Angie, you're my best friend. What's wrong?"

Angie shook her head, but it was no use resisting Connie. If she stayed, she'd spill it all out. She jumped up. "Gotta go."

"Come back, Angie."

But Angie was already through the door and running across the yard.

Hours later she gave up trying to sleep. She could run away from Connie, but she couldn't outrun herself. She turned on the light in her peaceful bedroom and tried to read. The words blurred on the page. What if she told Connie and Connie laughed? Or worse, believed her? Angie cringed. Could she chance losing her best friend? On the other hand, if she didn't tell, there was already a yawning crack between them that could grow into an unbridged chasm.

"I couldn't tell her without dissolving into a puddle," she confessed to her shadowy, mirrored image across the room. The faint reflection gravely nodded understandingly. "But I could write a letter."

Fifteen minutes later Angie reread what she'd poured onto paper.

Dear Connie,

I couldn't tell you what was bothering me this afternoon. Now it's two o'clock, and I can't sleep. This isn't easy, but the reason I can't be a Teen Aide with you is that I'm a jinx.

Before you laugh or think I'm crazy, let me tell you some of the things that have happened. My dad called me Jinx and then he died. I began wondering if he could be right. At first I thought it was just a coincidence, and I guess I still do, but so many other things have happened!

Right after Dave Jackson told me he liked me a lot, he got hurt. Then you came. At first I wasn't going to be your friend because of what could happen. But I thought since you were so strong and you carry your "guide," it would be OK. Then you got sick.

I know you're going to tell me to forget it. I know I ought to. God doesn't want us even to think such things, because they aren't true! My mind says that. Yet every time my heart is about ready to believe it too, something happens, and I get all hot and cold wondering if I attract bad luck.

Your idea about being a Teen Aide is terrific, and I'd love to. I can't, though. All those poor sick people—maybe I'd be so nervous I'd do something terrible.

Even though I know you'll never be able to

*understand completely, I hope you'll be able to
accept me the way I am.*

Your Jeff

Mentally exhausted, Angie hastily searched out
an envelope, addressed it to Connie, and tiptoed to
the front porch. The mailman would pick up their
outgoing mail first thing in the morning, and Connie would get the message before school ended.

If the previous day had seemed long, this one
grew into an eternity. Angie alternated between
being glad she'd written the letter and mentally
kicking herself for having done so. What would
Connie think? Would she be so disgusted she'd
look for another Jeff? She'd have no trouble.
Connie was already one of the best-liked freshman
girls.

The interminable day closed at last. Angie
wished the bus would either hurry or break down
completely. The suspense of not knowing what lay
ahead lay so heavily on her heart that she wished
it were all over one way or another.

She saw no sign of life across the street.
Windows were closed in spite of the Indian summer afternoon. Angie sighed and turned into her
own yard. Something white fluttered from the
door.

"Aunt Ida insisted I lay down *on my bed* while
she went grocery shopping. Come over immediately," the note in Connie's scrawl read. It was
signed *Mutt.*

Angie dropped her books on the porch, hesitantly crossed their yards. A second note, this one
on the front door of the house, told Angie to walk
in and go on upstairs to Connie's room.

What's a nice girl like you doing in a place like this?" Angie forced a laugh and a wave as she entered Connie's bedroom.

"Waiting for you." Connie didn't respond to Angie's pretended lightheartedness. She swung her long legs over the edge of the bed and made room for Angie to sit down. Then she just looked at her friend for a long, long time.

"I guess you read my letter." Angie shivered. Why didn't Connie say something?

Unexpected tears spilled from Connie's eyes. "You should have told me sooner, Angie. It must have been terrible for you to think such a thing about yourself."

Angie gasped. Of all the reactions, this was one she hadn't expected!

"I was scared to tell you," she confessed. "No one knows, not even Mom, although sometimes I think she suspects." She laced her fingers together. "Oh, Connie, you don't know what it's been like!" The dam of misery so long buried inside suddenly broke. "Always wondering if I really am some kind of weirdo. Feeling guilty, because I know a Christian shouldn't feel like this. Afraid to tell anyone." Something hot and wet slid down her face.

"I do know, Angie." Connie's quiet answer stopped her outburst.

"How? I mean—" she stumbled, the memory of what Aunt Ida told her rushing past her own problems.

Connie looked out the window. Angie knew she wasn't seeing the Trescott home with colored leaves blowing on the lawn, but a faraway country. "I fight fear every day." She turned back to Angie and managed a small, unusual grin. "That's why I act so crazy sometimes. It's not as bad as it used to be, though."

Angie could only listen, stunned by the pain in Connie's voice.

"I know exactly what it's like. From the minute I learned my folks were being transferred to Africa, I rebelled. Dad had only one year left in the service. Why did the Army have to send him there? Why couldn't they just have given him a job somewhere to finish out his time?" Tears sparkled on the long dark lashes so in contrast with her blonde hair. "My folks didn't try to play down the danger. Right now Americans, especially the military, can be a target overseas. Dad just said, 'The good Lord must have a reason for us to go.' It didn't help much then." She swallowed.

"How did you make it better?" Angie twisted a fold of the bedspread and held her breath.

"First, I had my guide." Connie reached for the worn Testament on her bedside table. "I am not superstitious, and I don't believe the book has any power in itself. It's what is *inside* that's important. But just touching it reminds me that God is still in control." Her solemn expression dissolved into a laugh. "Also, once I 'faced the dragon' it wasn't so bad."

Intrigued, Angie's eyes opened wide. "What do you mean by 'face the dragon'?"

Connie laughed again. "When I was 5, a dragon lived in my closet."

"Sure it did!" Angie was grateful for the lessening of tension in the room.

"As far as I was concerned, it did. No matter how much Dad or Mom told me different, or threw back the door and showed me the closet was empty, I knew the dragon was there, hiding in a pocket by becoming smaller or something. When they left the room, the dragon got big again. One day Mom sat me down and told me make-believe was fine as long as I knew it was make-believe. Pretending could be fun. But it wasn't pleasing to Jesus if I let it seem real." Connie's eyes grew shadowy, and Angie knew she was reliving that long-ago day when she was 5.

"I knew she was right. The hardest thing I ever did was to wait until she left my room, then go *alone* and open the closet door! Before I did, I asked God to help me not be scared."

Angie closed her eyes. She could see a scared, 5-year-old Connie asking God for help, then timidly approaching her closet. "Did He?"

"Not the way I expected. My heart pounded. My hands felt sweaty. But God gave me the courage to face my invisible dragon. I yanked open the closet door. I searched every corner, pants pocket, and coat. I looked into every box, still half expecting something to jump out." She paused. "When I walked away from the closet that afternoon, I knew there was no dragon except in my mind."

"How did you face the dragon of being scared about your folks?" Angie prodded.

"The same way. First I just asked God to take away the fear. He didn't. It stayed like a lump of ice. Then I realized it was going to take some action on my part to make my prayers effective. The more I read the Bible and was reminded how much God loved me, the less I demanded that He miraculously bring my folks home right away.

"Mom wrote that when they got to their quarters, they discovered a struggling group of Christians who were so discouraged they were about to give up. Mom and Dad have been able to join them and encourage them."

"I don't understand," Angie said. "You told me you still fight fear every day. Once you faced your dragon, didn't it go away, like when you were little?"

"No. It never does." Connie pushed back her hair with one hand and looked straight at Angie. "God doesn't promise it'll be easy. Just that we won't be tried more than we can stand. There isn't a headline or a news item about Africa that doesn't send my heart scurrying into my throat." The expression in her eyes hurt Angie. "Then I have to do it all over—remind myself God has a plan for their lives and mine, and ask for strength to make it through. Each time it takes a little less time to settle down, but the fear is there ready to pounce if I let it."

"That's the way I've felt," Angie cried out. "Just when I start to get over things, something else comes along!"

"Sometimes the only way to combat it is to 'march up and throw open the closet door.'"

"Then you think I have to bring it all out in the open, my fears and everything?" Angie asked.

Connie's face clouded over. "I can't tell you what to do. I can only share what's worked for me. But since you've told me, don't you feel better?"

"Of course I do! I was so afraid you'd—" She bit her unsteady lips.

"Don't say it. I know exactly what you thought, and you were wrong." Connie flipped open her Testament. "Listen. Psalm 115:11 says, 'Ye that fear the Lord, trust in the Lord; he is their help and their shield.' If you ever want to find peace, get out a concordance and start looking up scriptures that promise freedom from fear. There are dozens of them." She turned pages. "This is one of my favorites. Psalm 91:5: 'Thou shalt not be afraid for the terror by night; nor for the arrow that flieth by day.'" Connie slowly closed the Testament. "I am glad my Testament has Psalms and Proverbs, too! Angie . . . " she stopped for so long that Angie wondered if she would finish the sentence.

"Nationals in some of the areas my father has to patrol still use arrows as weapons. That's why this verse means so much to me."

A rush of shame filled Angie. "Connie, I thought *I* had problems! I'm sorry I ever bothered you with them." She felt a sob rise in her throat.

"Don't ever be sorry." Connie swung toward her, and the little lamps behind her eyes turned them cobalt blue. "Anything important enough to concern you, *no matter how small,* is important to me. And even more important to God," she added reverently. With a sudden mood shift, Connie said in her best no-nonsense voice, "Enough about me. Let's work on your problem."

Angie was happy to agree. Even though she wouldn't have traded the glimpse into Connie's divided heart for anything else, it was heavy stuff. "What do you suggest?"

"Teen Aides," Connie said so promptly that Angie blurted out, "What's with you? Does your mind run double track?"

"Sure. That's how I get so much thinking done," Connie bragged, although a suspicious shine showed her eyes still held unshed tears. "Now, are you going to face your dragon, open your closet door, and all that?"

Doubt gripped Angie, but she obediently replied, "You bet your sweet tootsies I am."

"Sweet tootsies! What's that?"

"Sheer relief," Angie told her loftily and scrambled off the bed. "Lead on, Lieutenant Gregory."

"Give me a few more days, and I'll do just that."

The weekend passed in a kaleidoscope of church services, studying, getting Connie briefed on what she'd missed at school, and plans for new teen activities at church. Mutt and Jeff were involved in the special outreach activities, and Angie's birthday party had fired the opening gun, Connie told Angie.

"There's no reason those kids at school won't start coming to youth group activities and services," she eagerly said. "Look how much fun they had at your party."

"I can hardly wait for snow and a trip to Mount Hood. Have you ever skied? I'll probably fall down the whole mountain."

"They only let you on little bunny slopes to start," Connie reassured her. "I went a few times when we lived in Vermont one winter, and they are really careful about seeing that you don't do anything dangerous."

"At least we have a nice hospital if I break my leg," Angie muttered, but she grinned when Connie glared at her.

Several days passed before Connie and Angie could see the hospital supervisor in charge of Teen Aides. School went on as usual. Mutt and Jeff stayed inseparable, yet never so involved with one another they didn't have time to welcome others. Angie loved the feeling of a smaller school. The ones she had attended before coming to Indian River had given her the feeling of "nobodyness" as she called it—just another number on the rolls. Here there was a chance to be involved, even as a freshman. There wasn't nearly so much class consciousness. In order to have a good band and choir and drill team, everyone willing to participate was needed.

One early October morning *the day* arrived. Angie had circled it in red on her calendar. She and Connie were to see Mrs. Harper at 3:30 sharp.

"I hope she isn't," irrepressible Connie said as the two girls scuffled through fallen leaves, making brilliant patches on the gray pavement and fading lawns.

"Who isn't what?" Angie couldn't always shift gears fast enough to keep up with Connie's startling half sentences.

"Mrs. Harper. I hope she isn't," Connie repeated, then howled at Angie when she caught on and grimaced before laughing.

Harper by name but not by nature, Angie thought when they were ushered into the supervisor's compact office. The efficient capped nurse across the desk from them was middle-aged, trim, and businesslike, but not the nagging type.

"Why do you want to be a Teen Aide?" were her first words after they were seated.

Connie answered readily enough. "I've wanted to be a nurse for a long time; and after I was here for my appendectomy, I wanted it even more. This way I can get the feel of the hospital."

"And you?" The friendly voice dispelled some of Angie's fears.

"I'm not sure." She had to be honest with this woman she knew could become a real friend. "First it was because Mu—Connie wanted me to." She hesitated.

"And?" Mrs. Harper wouldn't let her get away with such a feeble reason.

"I think it's because I'd like to feel I am really useful to someone." The last words were barely a whisper.

Mrs. Harper evidently caught them. "That's good enough for me. Although you'll have to fill out some rather lengthy forms, you have a good chance of being selected. We need two new aides."

"It isn't because Aunt Ida and Angie's mom work here, is it?" Connie asked hesitantly.

"No! We never select Teen Aides according to relatives. You'll have to pass physical exams, be considered along with two others who have applied, and then go through an orientation period." She rose and smiled. "Report back here this time next week, and we'll see what we can do for you."

"How did you dare ask what you did?" Angie held the outside door open for Connie and they stepped back into the hazy October afternoon. As long as she lived she'd associate burning autumn leaves with this moment. The Columbia swept by on its way to the Pacific, small whitecaps dancing along on the water. Spruce, pine, cedar, and fir sent probing fingers into the blue sky, and church spires pointed the way to heaven.

"I had to. I wouldn't want us to get on because

of Aunt Ida and your mom." Connie slowed a bit. Her white skimmers shone, and her pastel striped dress only intensified her blue eyes.

Angie knew she too looked nice. The candy pink cotton skirt and matching T-shirt added color to her usually pale face. "Do you think we'll get picked?"

"Why not?" Connie struck a ridiculous pose. "Who else is better qualified than two such charming girls? By the way," she giggled. "I thought I'd choke when you almost called me Mutt to Mrs. Harper!"

"Me too. You notice I covered it, though."

"Yeah, and besides, behind all that starchy businesslike outside I'll bet Mrs. Harper has one terrific sense of humor. She'd have to, to help run a hospital."

Angie cast an affectionate glance behind them at the low building sprawling against the trees. "Funny, now that I know I may be part of it, it doesn't seem as scary. Guess 'facing the dragon' either abolished him or at least shrunk him!"

Exactly a week later, two eager girls presented themselves to Mrs. Harper. She didn't keep them waiting. "Good news and congratulations." She held a hand out to each.

Angie could see what Connie had discerned earlier. There was a real twinkle in the dark eyes that could bore into a person when she wanted answers. Strangely enough, it was Connie who got rattled. "You mean we're really in?"

Angie hadn't known until that instant how terribly important it was to Connie, or how she'd evidently been vanquishing some dragons of doubt and possible disappointment the past week.

"Yes. And we're glad to have you." Mrs. Harper gripped their hands, then walked to a sliding door, reached inside and pulled out two hangers. Sunny yellow and spotless white combined in a small stripe to make the jumper-type dresses with full skirts and straps crossed in back.

"Why, they aren't pink and white!" *What possessed her to say that?* Angie wondered. Would Mrs. Harper be offended? "I mean, I like the yellow a lot better. I just always thought candy-stripe uniforms were pink and white."

Mrs. Harper laughed, crinkle lines surrounding her dark eyes. "Yellow is my favorite color," she confessed in a conspiratorial whisper. "Patients feel more cheerful just looking at it. Besides, yellow goes well with our soft green walls and outdoor paintings." She smiled. "You'll need to wear short sleeved white blouses with your uniforms, and later you'll want cardigan sweaters. White." She glanced at the girls' skimmers. "Get white, rubber-soled shoes. Three or four hours on your feet can make them pretty tired."

"When do we start?" Connie had never looked prettier than with soft color in her lightly tanned face.

"Your school has a teachers' in-service day next week. Monday, isn't it?" Mrs. Harper consulted her calendar. "Come in then, and I'll see that you're given a complete guided tour, then instructed about your duties."

Angie walked out, carefully holding her uniform. "She sure knew how to pick for size. This looks perfect." She could feel excitement pouring through her. Ever since that long, serious talk with Connie, things hadn't seemed so overwhelming. Was her jinx broken at last? Or if there never had been a jinx, and she was starting to really believe that, maybe she was growing up and leaving her dragon behind.

6

"Put on the whole armour of God . . .'" Pastor Jennings read.

Angie jerked her attention back to the present. Fall sunlight streamed in through the windows of the small church. *Small, but beautiful,* Angie thought, running a contented gaze over the woodpaneled walls. *Simple, but effective.* And the people! Never had she seen such enthusiastic, happy Christians. Pastor Jennings went on, light falling on his silver-streaked hair. "'Wherefore, take unto you the whole armour of God, that ye may be able to withstand in the evil day . . .'"

Angie found herself listening carefully as the different pieces of armor were mentioned: "'girt about with truth; . . . breastplate of righteousness; . . . feet shod with the preparation of the gospel of peace; above all, taking the shield of faith. . . . And take the helmet of salvation, and the sword of the Spirit, which is the word of God.'"*

Why, that's what Connie did! She carried the "sword of the Spirit" everywhere she went. "I'm going to get me a 'sword of the Spirit' too," Angie decided. "There's plenty of room in my new Teen Aide jumper pocket for a small Testament." Warmth flowed through her when she remembered how, when she'd donned the becoming jumper over a crisp white camp shirt, she had felt she was putting on armor, just as Pastor Jennings said.

Angie concentrated on the service. The sermon was good; but then, it always was. Yet a tiny part of her mind remembered another service, a private one. After their acceptance interview with Mrs. Harper, Connie had turned to Angie. For once, she didn't try to hide her feelings with a joke. "Angie, this is such a special moment. Couldn't we have a

---

*Ephesians 11:17.

little thankful time to mark it?"

"Why, sure." Angie wasn't too sure what she meant but wasn't long in finding out. Connie led the way to a stand of virgin timber, untouched by logging, crisscrossed with trails where the Indian River people took walks and their kids played. A whispering stream ran through it, and Connie stopped on the pine-needle-covered ground next to the stream. "Let's bow our heads and make this a time to remember."

She didn't wait for Angie's answer; she just prayed, "Dear God, we're thankful You are going to let us be Teen Aides. We realize it's an honor and a challenge. Help us to reflect the light of Your Son and our Saviour Jesus Christ. Amen."

Angie had never felt closer to Connie. After a minute she huskily added, "Dear God," but no more words would come. It had been years since she'd prayed out loud. She finally said, "In Jesus' name, amen."

Connie squeezed her hand, and they silently left the secluded spot. It wasn't until much later that Connie said, "You know, your prayer is acceptable. God hears what our hearts say," then she turned the subject to Teen Aides.

Now Angie thought of the look on Connie's face. Although everyone knew what Connie stood for, she didn't go around preaching. Or did she? Wasn't living her life the way she did the best sermon of all? One of the junior boys had commented when Angie walked past his locker, "That Connie Gregory is quite a girl. More fun than anyone, but she never compromises her ideals, if you know what I mean." The same warm feeling

Angie had then filled her now.

I'm going to be more like Connie so people will think that about me, she thought. *No, I'm going to be more like Jesus. Connie said once never to pattern yourself after another person, even a good friend or family member. If you do, they might let you down, and your faith could shatter. How does she know so much? Maybe from being all over the country, even the world, on Army bases. Like she said, she had to carry her happiness with her, and her faith, too.*

Connie stirred uneasily next to Angie, shot her a quick smile, and turned her attention back to Pastor Jennings.

"God calls us to be our best," he was saying. "He gave His best, and He expects us to do our best, whatever that is. God never expected Abraham Lincoln to do what Madame Curie did. He doesn't expect you to do anything except be your very own best, to take the free gift of salvation, develop it, and share it with others."

Angie listened hard. Funny he should choose something so in line with her own thoughts.

"It has been said Jesus Christ's greatest credential was Himself. Not what He *did,* His miracles such as raising the dead, but what He *was.* My prayer is that each of us may discover who and what he is, then work with all his might to fulfill his God-given potential for Him."

When Angie awoke early Monday morning, too excited to sleep, she thought of the sermon. Cuddling back in her soft bed, glad for time to think, she determined to do just what Pastor Jennings had said. "God made me the way I am," she whispered to her quiet room. "He knows all about me. Oh, I *want* to give my best and be free forever of worrying about myself!" A lone tear escaped, but Angie brushed it away. "God, please guide Connie and me. Amen."

"How do I look?" Connie bounced into the Trescott front door a little after eight. They were to be at the hospital at nine, and Mom would drive them; then they planned to walk home afterward, stopping at the Snack Shack for a treat. Connie twirled around. "Aren't I *great?*" Her eyes fixed on Angie. "Wow! You look like a real doll in that outfit!"

Angie could feel herself turn scarlet although she knew there was some truth in what Connie said. When she'd looked at the ecstatic girl in the mirror this morning, she'd noticed flags of color flying in her cheeks and how her shining brown hair blended with the yellow-striped jumper.

"Did you eat any breakfast?" Connie demanded.

"Not much." Angie made a face. "Too excited, I guess."

"March yourself to that table and—hey, do I really see blueberry muffins?" Connie pretended to stagger. "Could a starving—well, a not-quite-full—neighbor have one or two?"

"Of course." Mom laughed at Connie's exuberance, and even Angie went back to the table and managed a second muffin. "You girls are going to have a workout, so you'd better fortify yourselves."

"Workout? What do you mean by that?" Connie mumbled through her muffin.

"You're getting the full tour, then you'll be

given a final briefing. Take notebooks. There's a lot to remember."

Angie switched from hot to cold and back again when Mom let them out in front of the hospital. She was glad she'd snatched up a heavy white sweater bought for just such crisp mornings.

"Don't look as if you're going to the gallows," Connie ordered, but Angie caught the quiver in her voice.

"You're just as nervous as I am," she hissed. Somehow it made her feel better. It must be true that misery really does love company! That thought cheered her. After all, the hospital wouldn't let her do anything to hurt anyone.

Mrs. Harper made that quite clear. "I'm taking the morning off so I can show you around person-ally," she told them. Her dark eyes sparkled. "We're pretty proud of this hospital, I can tell you that."

"I've always wondered why Indian River has its own hospital," Angie timidly confessed. "I mean, it's not all that far to Portland, and they have a lot of good hospitals."

"It's far when someone's badly hurt," Mrs. Harper told them. "We're a lot closer to Mount Hood. We also get patients from car accidents in the Columbia Gorge. You haven't lived here long enough to know how icy the roads can be in winter. Many times those extra miles into Portland could make the difference between life and death."

Even Connie was impressed. "I never thought of that."

"A lot of people didn't. That's why it took educating the public about 10 years ago when some of us saw the desperate need for medical facilities in Indian River." Mrs. Harper pushed open a door marked *Employees Only.* "We'll start with our kitchen."

Angie looked at the shining stainless-steel equipment, the racks and pans and stoves.

"No microwaves here," Mrs. Harper laughed. "Although they are convenient, we believe in cooking with time and love. Besides," she motioned to a heavy-set woman with lined face and broad smile, "Anna says she likes the old ways."

"I just learned to bake biscuits in an electric stove," Anna laughed along with Mrs. Harper until her eyes almost disappeared in crinkles. "I was used to a wood stove because we lived without electricity in the mountains—I'm too old to get along with newfangled gadgets." Her hands never faltered with the massive pile of dough. "You girls come back at lunch and try my cinnamon rolls."

Angie could feel her mouth water at the thought. Connie had told her how unusual and good the hospital food was, especially Anna's cinnamon rolls.

"She's an expert cook and takes pride in her work," Mrs. Harper bragged and herded the girls back into the hall. Angie remembered what Pastor Jennings had said about being the best. Anna was evidently doing just that!

Wards, just a peep into ICU ("intensive care unit," Mrs. Harper explained), offices, even the supply closets. Angie felt her head reel, and her fingers flew making notes of the location of the various rooms.

"We can handle 25 patients in wards and semiprivate rooms," she told them. "We can take another five in private rooms. Once after a chain reaction accident in the Gorge, we had 50 patients. They lined the halls until we could sort out those who only needed first aid, those who had to be transferred to Portland, and those we could care for here. There are five doctors in town who send patients here whenever necessary and take turns being on call day and night."

Connie caught Angie's look, and Angie knew she was thinking of what she'd said about being a doctor.

"You probably already know we have six regis-tered nurses, RNs, for our three shifts. We also have a half-dozen practical nurses who work part-time or are on the call board. Once in a great while every nurse and doctor we can lay our hands on is needed." A shadow crossed Mrs. Harper's face. "Pray to God that isn't necessary."

Some of Angie's enthusiasm dampened, and she saw that Connie had also grown silent. This wasn't a new sport or game. This was their en-trance into a world of reality. Would they measure up?

Angie was glad when they finished the tour and went back to Mrs. Harper's office. Connie voiced the question uppermost in their minds, "Where do we fit in?"

"Everywhere!" Mrs. Harper's eyes twinkled when they gasped. "Really, we use you all over the place. Not for patient care, though." She leaned back in her chair. Angie suspected she had learned the art of taking a moment's relaxation when she could.

"You will come in one afternoon a week," Mrs.

Harper said. She reached for a squared-off chart on her desk. "I suppose you'd like to be together. Mutt and Jeff usually are." She looked as if she enjoyed their surprise. "Oh yes, there isn't much I don't find out about my girls."

A little glow at the words "my girls" made Angie sit up straighter.

"I'd like you from four until seven-thirty or eight on Tuesdays if that's all right with your school schedule."

"Fine," they chorused.

"Later, when you've been here longer, I'll see about changing to six to nine, during visiting hours, but the earlier shift is a good learning place. Connie, I'm going to start you out as a messenger. You'll float between offices and wards, do whatever the charge nurse tells you. You'll assist wheelchair patients coming in and out, work with flowers, and so on.

"Angie, you've already taken a semester of typing, haven't you?"

"Yes." *What does typing have to do with Teen Aides?* she wondered.

"We need help in our public relations/business office. I'd like you to work with our small clerical staff in filing, light typing, and so on."

Angie didn't know whether she was relieved or disappointed. She'd dreaded being put where she'd be around patients, yet Connie's work sounded a lot more interesting. But she merely said, "Thank you, Mrs. Harper," and let it go at that.

"Eventually you'll do every job a Teen Aide can be given," their supervisor explained. She abandoned her relaxed pose. "Now comes the most important part: our rules for Teen Aides. I'll give you a printed sheet to study, but I also want to discuss them. Remember, these rules are exactly that—rules. You will neither break nor bend them. If you ever do, you could put yourself or others in grave danger."

Angie shivered and pulled her sweater closer around her shoulders.

"Under no circumstances are you ever to give a patient anything to eat or drink unless directly ordered to do so by your charge nurse," Mrs. Harper said.

"Not even a drink of water?" Connie's eyes were round.

Mrs. Harper shook her head. "No! Water can be dangerous to a postoperative patient. Even a seemingly well person may be ordered to stay off water for tests. You may be asked to get water. *Don't do it.*" She waited to let it sink in. "Next, if you ever see anything that even appears to be out of the ordinary, tell your charge nurse immediately."

"C—can you give us some examples?" Angie asked.

"A patient slumped in a chair or with eyes closed. He or she could very well be asleep, but never assume anything. Don't touch the patient, just get a nurse to check. It's better to cry 'wolf' than to let anything slide that could be a problem. Visitors also sometimes smuggle in food and even liquor if they think they can get away with it. If you ever have reason to suspect a patient has something harmful or that he or she isn't supposed to have, *report it.*"

Mrs. Harper's eyes sharpened. *"Prevention* is

the word we use in Indian River Community Hospital. Especially when you're 'floating' with fewer duties than the nurses, you are in an excellent position to keep two outsize eyes open to what's going on."

"It's a big responsibility, isn't it?" Connie commented.

"Yes, it is. It's also one of the most worthwhile challenges you will ever have. A few of our girls only see that they are given what can be considered 'minor' jobs, Connie, Angie." Those all-seeing eyes searched each in turn. "If nuts and bolts could think they might consider their jobs small. But where would great machines be without them? I can't over stress the fact every single person who serves this hospital—and most important, the patients who come here—is vitally necessary." After a few seconds she asked, "Any questions?"

The hundreds of things Angie wanted to know had fled in front of Mrs. Harper's challenge to them. Angie's heart beat fast under the crisp, new uniform. Did she dare? She drew in her breath and before she could change her mind asked, "Have you ever had to—to fire a Teen Aide?" The minute it was out, she realized how out of place her question was in the quiet office. She watched Mrs. Harper's smile slowly fade before she answered. "Yes, Angie. Now and then we get a girl who simply can't take her job seriously. When that happens, we have to let her go." Sadness dulled the usually bright eyes. "Now, if you don't have any other questions, let's go sample those cinnamon rolls."

Angie saw Mrs. Harper straighten her shoulders and the effort it cost her to smile. Deep inside another pledge formed. *As long as I am a Teen Aide, I won't make her look like that.* Then, *God, will You help me, please?*

7

Angie stood at her window looking into a whipped-cream world. "Mom, it's been snowing!" Excitement tingled from head to toe as she stared at the billows and mounds and heaps of snow. "There must be a foot of it!" Mom came in, sleepily rubbing her eyes. "Isn't it lovely? It's been years since I saw snow, and you haven't ever seen more than a few flakes or drizzly stuff that isn't worthy of the name snow."

Angie was already rooting in her closet for the new boots and parka Mom had given her for her birthday. Before she found them, Connie's special *rat-a-tat-tat* was followed by a soft thud against Angie's window where a loosely formed snowball had splattered.

Angie raced across her room and heedless of the cold, threw the window wide. Wow, it felt freezing! The lightweight PJs she'd brought from California were no match for Oregon winters.

"Come on out, lazybones!" Connie tossed up another handful of snow. Her hair shone from the hood of a ski jacket, and her sparkling blue eyes reflected the sun. "School's been canceled. Something about the boiler. We have a whole wonderful day!"

Angie could hear Mom talking with Connie in the kitchen while she scrambled into her blue jacket and pants. Every memory of winter scenes she'd seen on posters or TV faded before the reality of Indian River in winter. Still yanking at her parka zipper, she tore downstairs, feeling 5 instead of 15.

The girls couldn't wait for breakfast, and Mom finally agreed to hold it off for an hour. "That will give me time for something special," she promised.

Angie followed Connie into a picture postcard yard. "Look! Even the pickets have caps. And Connie—" her voice failed her at the sheer beauty.

Stately fir- and spruce- and pine-bowed branches frosted with heavy icing. A deep turquoise sky spread like a painted ceiling. Sunshine's exploring fingers stroked the landscape. Lazy smoke drifted from chimneys, and everywhere colorful figures of small to large sizes tumbled into the street.

"It's so gorgeous it hurts." Connie brushed one finger over wet eyelashes and left snowflakes from her mitten. "Come on!"

Except for short stops for a popover breakfast, a long-simmered vegetable-soup-with-dumplings late lunch/early dinner, and a few trips inside to warm cold fingers, Angie and Connie spent the whole day outside.

"I can't believe the feeling of community," Angie whispered early that evening. *"Everybody's* here and having fun together."

"I know what you mean," Connie whispered back. "It's what I've always wanted, a sense of belonging."

The wistful echo in her own heart brought a lump to Angie's throat. She turned her back to the gigantic blaze of wood piled up by half the people who had come to go sledding. Before her lay a packed sled run. Young and old had tramped the long, sloping hill until it was a snow-covered, hard-as-rock lane with just enough turns before the long, smooth run that ended in a meadow. Angie had been down dozens of times. Each rush through the chill air sent her heart to her mouth, but she could hardly wait to climb up and go again. Every conceivable means of transportation went down the hill, and Angie had been on most of them. Plastic dishpans, snowshovels, inner tubes, sleds—

homemade and "store-boughten," as she had heard one youngster say a little scornfully.

And the people! Laughing couples, scores of children; young marrieds carefully putting tiny ones in their laps; the town banker, whose portly frame looked quite funny sitting upright on a sled; grandparents showing they certainly weren't out of the running.

"Race you," she challenged Connie, who stood munching on a potato that had been baked in foil in the fire.

"You're on." Connie turned to a couple of neighbor boys stuffing toasted marshmallows into already-grimy faces. "Is it OK to use your sleds?"

"Sure." The boys pointed to matching red and blue flyers standing upended on their runners so the seats could dry from the fire.

"Blue to match my jacket." Angie pulled the sled to the hilltop and flung herself down on it.

"Red to match—" Connie scratched her head trying to think of a comeback. "I know. Red for the winning sled." She laughed impudently and poised. "Ready, set, *go!*"

Angie flattened out on the sled, steered toward the right, and shoved off. The name on the sled was right. It was really a flyer. She was aware of Connie beside her, a red-and-yellow streak.

"Come on, poky," Connie yelled and turned her laughing face toward Angie.

"Connie, watch out!" Angie screamed back.

Connie jerked her gaze back down the sled run. Directly in front of her lay an overturned plastic dishpan with a small boy picking himself up. He hadn't been visible from the top.

In that instant, Connie jerked the red flyer hard to the left, skimmed past the upset—and crashed.

Angie desperately tried to drag her feet, but succeeded only in dangerously tilting the sled. All she could do was finish the run. By the time she slowed and could leap off to start running back up the side of the slope, she was sobbing and gasping for breath. Why had she challenged Connie? Everything had been going so well! Only a few minor things like rain the day of the freshman pep rally she and Connie had helped plan for outdoors, but nothing big. Working as a Teen Aide had almost erased the feeling of being bad luck. Now this!

Connie had taken a terrible spill to avoid the boy. What if she—? Angie clamped down hard on the thought. "God," she prayed, "please . . . " She could see a group of concerned neighbors and townspeople gathered around the crash site. No one was moving. Everyone was just looking down. Angie's heart turned to ice, and she tried to run faster. "Is she—?"

"She's fine."

Blessed relief flooded through Angie and she dropped to the snow next to Connie. "Are you really OK?" She held her breath and waited for Connie to reply.

"Just a mouthful of snow," Connie sputtered, trying to brush her face clear. "I went in headfirst!" The crowd laughed at her rueful comment. She leaned over the sled. "Oh, Jimmy's steering gear is bent, too."

"I can fix that easily," someone volunteered, then a big man lifted Connie to her feet, asking, "Sure you're all right?"

"You bet." Connie stood up and let him brush off her powdery layers of snow. "Best place to have *an accident*"—she stressed the word and her eyes bored into Angie—"is right here where it's soft." She grinned again, and the crowd scattered.

Angie couldn't move. "Why did I ever ask you to race?" she cried. She still felt shaken, although Connie looked normal enough.

"Big deal. We've been racing and playing all day, haven't we?" Connie's eyes widened and darkened until they almost glowed in the dim light. "You aren't getting back to that jinx stuff, I hope."

"N-not really, except when I was walking back up the hill," Angie confessed.

"I told you there would be ups and downs," Connie told her softly, facing Angie through the dusk. "You've had a lot of weeks of 'up.' A 'down' was bound to come." She tacked on, *"Down* was really the word for it! I've never felt so strange in my life as when I ended up with my face in a snowbank!" She gingerly touched her chin, and Angie saw a tiny streak. "Must have scratched myself. It will heal."

"No more sledding tonight." Angie set her chin firmly. "The run's getting too dark."

"One of the men said that tomorrow night they'll build a big fire at the bottom, too, and you can see the whole run."

Angie shivered, wondering if the chill was all from the air. "You really want to come back here with me?"

"Don't be a dummy. Of course I want to come back here with you," Connie mimicked. "Come on, let's go home. Mr. Reynolds said he'd give us a ride. He lives out past us."

Despite all the exercise, Angie found herself tossing and turning that night, remembering how Connie had jerked to the left then crashed. An unwelcome little whisper inside her taunted, *Is it starting all over?* Angie resolutely put it out of her mind, said her prayers, and closed her eyes. Surprisingly enough, the next time she opened them a gray winter day peeked in through the window.

"Sledding again tonight!" the cry went through Indian River High. "Gotta make the most of it. Weatherman says no telling how long it will last."

Angie reluctantly got ready after she and Connie finished at the hospital and had supper. She steeled herself against the first trip down the hill and made sure it was with Connie and two others on one of the long bobsleds. The second was easier, and by the tenth or so run, Angie managed to approach the top of the slope without a qualm.

For four nights they sledded, then an unexpected warm wind the natives call a Chinook swept away every trace of snow except on the shining slopes of Mount Hood. Both girls would go skiing during the Christmas holidays. Until then, every morning Angie ran to her window to see if the snows had returned in the night.

One Tuesday when they finished their hospital shifts, Angie said hesitantly to Connie, "You know, I wish we could do something for Indian River. It's done a lot for me, like making me feel I have a real home."

"Me too," Connie agreed. "Any ideas?"

"One. It may not be all that great, but"—she

plunged in—"I saw posters that the Indian River stores would be open evenings the week before Christmas. Oh, I know a lot of people do most of their shopping in Portland, but I imagine mothers with small children and those who work would like to have an evening off."

"And?" Connie watched her curiously.

"Well, it just seems maybe we could do a real community service, plus plant a few seeds. Why couldn't we ask Pastor Jennings if we could have a child-care evening or maybe two or three?" Angie warmed to her idea. "We could ask at school as well as at church for other helpers. If parents knew we'd take care of children from a year or 2 old up through maybe 10, it seems it might be helpful. We could do it from, say, six to eight o'clock."

"That's terrific!" Connie began, but stopped short. "But what would we do with them?"

Angie had thought it all out before she mentioned it. "Divide them into age groups. Play games with them, then read Bible stories, sing songs, teach them choruses, stuff like that."

"And call ourselves Angie's Angels."

"Don't be silly." Angie's face flamed.

"Why not? It's your idea." Connie refused to give up her catchy title. Others agreed. Pastor Jennings thought it was a great idea and put Connie, Angie, Tom Colver, and Lance Graham in charge of organizing it. The church ladies promised to make cupcakes and fruit punch. The youth group volunteered, and their enthusiasm brought in others from school who said they'd help. A few days later, posters sprouted all over Indian Creek.

A CHRISTMAS GIFT TO THE COMMUNITY

ANGIE'S ANGELS
will provide safe, fully supervised child-care
on Monday, Tuesday, and Wednesday nights,
December 21-23, 6:00 to 8:00 p.m.
No charge. Community service. Ages 1-10.

Name and address of the church followed, with Angie and Connie's as well as Pastor Jennings' telephone numbers for further information.

The news ran like a forest fire. Suddenly Angie Trescott and Connie Gregory were headlines. Connie faithfully replied, "It was all Angie's idea. I'm just a peon slave!"

For the first time since Dad had died, Angie felt completely happy. If now and then a niggling little doubt crept into her mind, she squashed it the way she would a poisonous bug. She was prettier, too. Her mirror told her so. Self-confidence from the praise given for her idea, as well as new assurance that God was helping her fight her battles, showed in her formerly sad face.

Never had she been busier! It was remarkable how many times Tom and Lance felt it necessary to get together with the girls, usually at Connie's since Mom still worked nights. Finally Angie admitted, "I think they have ulterior motives. Lance asked if I'd go to the holiday church banquet with him."

"And Tom asked me," Connie said. "I didn't know if Lance had gotten up the courage, so I didn't say anything sooner."

"Just think! We'll get to wear party dresses and everything!"

"That's not all," Connie told her, leaning across the table where they'd been studying. "A lot of the kids at school are thrilled and coming! Sarah Dobson ran up to me today, and I've never seen her so excited. 'I think it's great your church is sponsoring a dress-up banquet!' she told me. She said that those kids who just aren't into dancing never get to do things that let them wear pretty new dresses. Her boyfriend is even getting her an orchid corsage. And Sarah is a senior! Can you beat it?"

"I can hardly wait." Angie's eyes danced. "Mom says we can go to Lloyd Center in Portland. I know what I want—a frothy pale yellow with white lace."

"I want pink," Connie sounded ecstatic. "I love the ruffles and frills and feminine dresses just now. We're double-dating."

"I probably couldn't have gone otherwise. This is my very first real date with a boy coming to pick me up and everything." Angie giggled. "I sure hope I don't drop my fork or spill anything. I decided on yellow and white because of our aide uniforms."

"It will be perfect on you," Connie reassured. "And you won't spill. You're 15 years old, remember?" She ducked her head. "I'm just as nervous as you are. I've never had a real date either. I'm glad Tom and Lance are so nice. They're probably even more nervous than we are!"

Angie thought of Connie's evaluation when she opened the door to Lance the night of the banquet. His blond hair looked great against his dark suit and white shirt, but his gray eyes were anxious, then admiration crept into them. "Hey, you don't look like the girl who threw snowballs at me a few weeks ago!"

It broke the ice. Literally. Angie knew she'd never looked nicer. The soft yellow had to be her best color. She accepted the box he held out, opened it, and saw tiny yellow and white rosebuds tied with silver ribbon. Her very first corsage!

"Connie tattled," Lance explained with a laugh. "Tom had a harder time for himself, and finally asked Mrs. Gregory what color Connie planned to wear."

Connie shimmered in rose pink. Her corsage was identical to Angie's except for pink rosebuds instead of yellow. Tom was as dark as Lance was blond, and he possessed a well-developed sense of humor. He kept them laughing all the way to the church.

Mrs. Jennings and her crew of workers had spared nothing to make the fellowship hall beautiful. Long white tables garbed in white tablecloths held crimson and emerald candles nestled among spicy fir branches. Red ribbons led from poinsettia centerpieces to each place, and the stainless steel cutlery sparkled in the candlelight.

Mom had been able to get the evening off, and she waved from the kitchen. Angie, feeling very grown up in her first long dress, took Lance over to speak with her. She'd wondered whether to get three-quarters or long but had decided she could always cut it off later if she needed to. In spite of its beauty, it was simple enough to wear to church in midsummer.

"Nothing short of a miracle," she mumbled to

Connie when the boys' backs were turned near the end of dinner. "I didn't spill!"

"What a dinner!" Connie leaned back in her chair with a satisfied smile. "The kids really ate, didn't they?"

"No one makes lasagna the way Aunt Ida does," Angie said. "Then that special salad with vegetables and the hot rolls and—"

"—and whipped strawberry dessert! If I hadn't been so stuffed, it wouldn't have bothered me at all to ask for seconds."

"When you swallow and it doesn't go anywhere, you know you're through," Angie told her heartlessly. She blushed when Lance turned back with a question, "Are you on the program?"

"Not me." She grinned. "I'm saving all my energy for next week and the influx of children!"

Someone struck a key on the piano, and the chattering group settled down to await the entertainment. To everyone's surprise, the local pharmacist, who had been asked to sing, turned out to have a beautiful voice. The enduring words of "O, Holy Night" swept into Angie's heart. She let her gaze travel around the room, resting especially on the nonchurch kids who had attended. Every face was turned toward the singer and in the flickering candlelight softness often hidden at school showed.

If only the whole world could know Jesus, Angie thought, blinking back tears. *Then the peace and perfectness of this moment could go on forever.* Did the others feel it? She couldn't help thinking they did. Some had been attending church more or less regularly since Connie's "opening gun," as she'd called Angie's surprise birthday party. Tonight even more had come. They would leave with more than a good time, remembering an excellent meal and warm fellowship. Pastor Jennings spoke only a few minutes, but he made clear that every person present needed to make room in his or her heart not only for the baby Jesus but for the resurrected Christ.

Thank You, God, Angie's silent prayer winged upwards. *For Your Son.*

8

Angie looked at Connie and burst into laughter. "Am I as big a mess as you are?" Her eyes whisked over her jeans and T-shirt.

"Worse! Why did every child here have to hug us *after* eating those frosted cupcakes?" Connie wanted to know. Her complaint turned to satisfaction. "You have to admit it—Angie's Angels was a great idea. Did anyone get a count?"

"Twelve on Monday night, 18 last night, and 16 tonight, although it felt like 126." Angie's glance took in the room of chattering children. Only a few moments remained of the three-night child-care program, and it had been a huge success. More than one mother had told them, "This was really a godsend! Dragging tired kids for last-minute shopping isn't my idea of fun."

"Will you have it next year?" one asked.

"Why, I don't know." Angie glanced at Connie and was amazed to see a strange look on her face. "Maybe if our pastor says OK."

"I hope so. Even if you had to charge for it, I'd be glad to pay."

Angie looked closely at the tired face and said impulsively, "I'm sure we wouldn't do it for money. It's been a great experience for all of us."

The shadowed eyes lit up. "Thank you. One of these weekends when I don't have to work, I'm going to try to come to church here. Any group, especially one that has teenagers so willing to knock themselves out for others, must be real Christians." She walked away, leaving the girls staring after her.

An hour later the two girls parted at Connie's door. Pastor Jennings had given them a ride home.

"Looks like we might get another snowstorm." Angie peered overhead at the scudding clouds and pulled her parka closer. "Brrr!" When Connie didn't respond, she asked, "Is something wrong?"

The bomb fell.

"I may have to go away," Connie told her.

"Go away! Where?" Angie felt as if someone had hit her hard.

"I got a letter from my folks. It made me all glad and sorry at the same time. Things are really tense where they are, and the Army is considering evacuating all personnel to a safer place—maybe back to France or Germany." Connie's voice reminded Angie of a too-tight violin string. "If they're moved, they'll probably want me with them. I want to be, but oh, Angie, for the very first time I'm in a place where I feel accepted. Where I'm someone other than just another 'Army brat' transferring from school to school!"

Angie stood stunned by the outburst. It was so unlike Connie to pour out her feelings this way. Angie felt as if Bonneville Dam had just burst and let the full force of the mighty Columbia River rush at her. "Would you have to go?"

"Probably not, but—" her voice failed.

Angie understood in a flash. Suppose it had been her mother and dad in such a situation. "Maybe they won't get transferred," she said, her voice small. Then she remembered that it could be dangerous if they weren't. She reached a small mittened hand and patted Connie's shoulder. "We'll just have to pray about it."

"I have been praying." Connie sounded desolate. "I've known since Monday but didn't want to say anything until after our Angie's Angels project was over." She straightened up and blew her nose on a tissue soggy from the damp, night air. "You better go on home before we both freeze. 'Night,

Angie." She turned and ran toward the porch.

Angie knew it was because Connie didn't want to cry in front of her. Some things were too private even to share with best friends. She slowly turned and trudged across the yard, unable to even get excited when the first snowflakes danced in the air and touched her flushed cheeks. What if Connie really did go? Laughing Connie, who had helped her begin to believe in herself. Who inspired her and reminded her of God's great love. Who went beyond friendship. Connie didn't just accept Angie the way she was. She helped her become all she could be.

Chilled to the bone, Angie hurried inside. Even a hot bath and her new warm, footed flannel PJs didn't touch the cold knot inside. She was glad when Mandrake sprang to her bed. Usually she pushed him off and told him to sleep on her bedside rug. Not tonight. She clutched his warm, black body close and wept into his soft fur. "What am I going to do without Connie?"

Mandrake meowed, crept closer, and purred his steady hum. She could feel his body vibrate, and at last the comforting sound lulled her to sleep. Just before she drifted off, she whispered, "At least I have you, Mandrake. I can't let Connie know how terrible I feel. Just you—and Jesus." Her heart formed a prayer her lips couldn't get out, jumbled, wanting Connie's folks to be safe but longing for Connie to stay in Indian River.

Mandrake had disappeared before she awakened to another sparkling white day. Some of Angie's fears in the night disintegrated before the crystal world outside her window. The slight shadow in Connie's eyes showed she hadn't slept much, but she acted as if everything were OK. "No sense getting all shook up before anything happens," she told Angie on the way to the bus stop, scuffing snow with her boots. "God knows what will happen, and I'm going to trust Him."

The firmness in her voice told Angie the subject was closed, at least temporarily. "Are you about ready for Christmas?" She turned the subject and was rewarded with a flash of gratitude from Connie's eyes.

"Almost. I can hardly wait for the caroling!"

Angie's heart lifted. Connie's faith must have come through with flags flying for her to sound so excited. "Same here. I'm glad the Teen Aides will get to do it. Can you imagine being in the hospital over Christmas? Ever since I was given floater duty and got over being terrified of what I might do when around the patients, I've thought of the holidays."

"I know." Connie idly grabbed a handful of snow and let its powder sift through her fingers. "Most of them will go home, all who possibly can. The others will be cared for by doctors and nurses who are willing to give some of their own time. Just going caroling doesn't seem like much, but the patients are already talking about it."

The bus rumbled to a stop, and there was no more time for confidences, but after school the two continued their conversation. Snow had deepened. If it kept falling, there would be a lot of fun during the holidays.

"I didn't get to tell you this morning," Angie

said, "but guess what I'm going to do Christmas afternoon after dinner."

"Visit with your mom, Aunt Ida, and me, naturally." Connie acted surprised.

Angie shook her head. She could feel the big grin starting. "Nope—I'm going to spend an hour at the hospital reading to Granny Hope. And guess what again." She didn't wait for an answer this time. "I'm taking my Bible."

"Granny Hope?" Connie gasped. Blue eyes stared in shock. "I thought she was an old—"

"Everyone thought so until one evening I found her crying." Angie clamped her lips shut, unwilling to betray everything that had happened that eventful evening. She substituted, "Anyway, I found out she's afraid of being blind. She has diabetes, you know. Granny finally broke down and said she hates TV and the hospital. It was so lonely, especially when the other bed in her room is empty. I asked if she'd like me to read to her. She said yes, and I did."

"But the Bible! With the kind of language she uses! How did you wangle that?"

Angie grinned even more. "A few days ago I said, 'Granny, if you'll let me choose what I want to read, I'll slip down for a little while on Christmas afternoon.'" Angie could remember the exact suspicious look on Granny's face.

"Well?" Connie impatiently demanded.

"She snorted. No other word for it. Snorted and told me that what I like couldn't possibly interest her. At first it turned me off, and I almost withdrew my offer. Then something in her eyes—well, anyway I stuck my chin out at the same angle as hers and asked, 'Don't you like love stories? The Bible is the greatest love story in the world, about how much God loves you. That's what I'd like to read.' She glared at me and finally mumbled, 'Well, I s'pose anything's better than being alone all Christmas Day. Bring your Bible and come on.'"

Angie's exact imitation of the troublesome old lady made Connie howl. They both laughed until they cried, and ever so often Connie would repeat, "Better than being alone!" and they'd get set off again. Finally Connie wiped her eyes. "I think you're neat, Angie Trescott. I'd have probably wanted to stick out my tongue or something even worse, even if I am 15 years old!"

Angie was still smiling when she unlocked the door and slipped into her own quiet home. The strange silence didn't dawn on her until she'd shucked off her damp clothes and stepped into comfortable jeans and a Mickey Mouse sweatshirt Connie had given her from a trip to Disneyland. Finally she realized an oppressive feeling in the house, a far cry from her joyous conversation with Connie. Had someone been in the house while they were gone? She searched the rooms but found nothing. Then it hit her—it wasn't an addition but something missing. Mandrake hadn't been at the door waiting for her. He hadn't cried for his dinner, either.

"Probably went out the cat door," she said out loud, but a worried little frown creased her forehead. "Mandrake. Mandrake, where are you?" she called. No answer. She stepped to the snow-clad patio and called again. No sleek black cat appeared.

"Funny. Since he's grown older he hates cold

weather." Angie shrugged. "He'll come when he's ready, I guess." As the evening passed she went to the door and called several times. Then she really began to get worried. Angie waited up for Mom and met her at the door with the words "When was the last time you saw Mandrake?"

"Why—" her mother struggled out of her storm coat and brushed snow out of her brown hair. "Not since early morning. Isn't he here?"

"No, and I've called and called."

"You know cats. People never own them. They own people! He'll turn up, probably in the morning." She hugged Angie. "Now get some sleep. Tomorrow's your last day before vacation."

Why did a feeling of dread keep step with Angie as she walked to her room? Memory of Mandrake's warm, purring body in her arms the night before haunted her, and her own words—*"at least I have you."* Some of her old fears returned. She'd let down her guard and learned to love Connie. Now Connie might have to leave. She'd clutched Mandrake close, maybe too close. Now he was gone. Permanently? She shuddered. It would be awful to lose the welcoming personality that filled home when she came in from school.

Mandrake didn't come back. Angie hid her fears from Mom, but she couldn't hide them from Connie. After the first couple days of vacation Connie wanted to know, "Why are you moping around?"

She caught Angie off guard. "I think I jinxed my cat."

"You jinxed a black cat?" Connie let out peals of laughter, doubling over until she almost rolled in a snowbank. "That has got to be the absolutely stupidest thing I have ever heard!"

Angie didn't laugh. She could feel tears of pain crawling up behind her eyes. Never in all their friendship had Connie failed to understand, even when she didn't agree with her.

Connie straightened. Angie saw the expression in her face when she looked at her. "I'm sorry. Really I am." Her humble voice ran over Angie's bruised heart like soothing lotion. "It isn't funny to you, is it?"

Angie shook her head, not trusting herself to speak.

Quick tears of sympathy sprang to Connie's eyes. "I'm the stupid one," she said fiercely.

"You aren't stupid." Angie gulped in a great breath of fresh, cold air. "And I guess it did sound pretty strange." The humorous side of it got to her at last, erasing some of the worry. "Here I thought I'd licked my problem, but it comes back every time I turn around!"

"Angie," Connie paused, as if afraid to go on. "Have you ever thought about talking with Pastor Jennings? About your problem, I mean."

"I couldn't!" Angie stepped back away from her and the suggestion. "He would probably think I was a candidate for the funny farm or something."

"God calls ministers to understand people," Connie said quietly. "Even though we know and trust in God and Jesus, sometimes it helps to share our worries, the way we've shared with each other." She got quiet then added, "I'm not wise enough to tell you how to get over this, but Pastor Jennings has had a lot of training to understand people and work with them." Angie started to say something, but Connie stopped her. "Don't answer. Just think about it. OK?"

Once the idea had been planted, it followed Angie the way Mandrake used to do. At first, the whole thing seemed impossible. Other times she seriously considered it. Was her problem big enough to add to all the other problems and burdens Pastor Jennings carried? Compared with the family who fought cancer, the girl with spina bifida, and all the rest of his flock? Why couldn't she just accept God's love and the impossibility of any kind of "jinx-ism"? Why couldn't she accept that life had the ups and downs Connie talked about—and that she wasn't responsible?

"Jesus, You walked before me," she prayed one night. "I know You must have been afraid some-times, too. At least I'm glad I can talk to You—no, *with* You, again. Is it silly to ask Your help about Mandrake?" A hot tear leaked from tightly shut lids. "It's just that the ones I love are always going away: Dad, Dave, maybe Connie—even my cat. Give me one more break, please. Amen."

Some of the peace and strength Angie longed for enveloped her a few nights later. Along with Connie, other Teen Aides, and any off-duty nurses available, a little procession formed at the end of the long hospital hall. Uniformed, some capped, bearing tall white candles in crystal holders, they began their carols, slowly going from one room to another, pausing to sing and wish the patients "Merry Christmas." The climax for Angie came in Granny Hope's room. At first the old woman's mouth stayed turned down, but when the group began "Silent Night," a slight smile formed on her lips. Granny's eyes searched the group, and Angie stepped around to the front, where she could be clearly seen.

Granny's eyes rested on her face. Angie could see an unaccustomed something sparkle in them. Was it the mere reflection of candle flames on tired eyes or something more, a silent asking for a human touch? Angie stretched out her hand, clasped the heavily veined, thin hand on the bedspread, and was amazed to feel a pressure of response.

Suddenly all the hours of volunteer work, often with her heart in her mouth, paid off. "I'll be in to read to you," Angie whispered. Again the emaciated fingers clutched hers, then a low voice said, "Good. Bring your Bible."

Through a mist the procession moved on, bringing hope to those with little hope, comfort and a time of peace to those in pain. "Would anyone like to have a cup of hot cocoa?" Mrs. Harper asked when they came from the last room. Angie had been amazed to see her there.

Connie and Angie looked at each other and shook their heads. Somehow sitting down and drinking cocoa would detract from the awe they felt after caroling.

"Aunt Ida's coming for us. Merry Christmas, everyone!" They escaped amid a shower of "Merry Christmas" greetings.

The small lobby was only half lighted, and the girls had a few moments together before Aunt Ida came. Angie watched a few more flakes sift down, then said, "Connie, if you still want me and if I still feel the same way after high school, there's nothing

I want more than to become a nurse." She bit her lip to keep from letting her emotions get out of control. "People say we'll change our minds a dozen times in school, but after tonight I don't think so."

Connie smiled at her but didn't speak.

"Even if you get sent off somewhere, let's plan to go to the same school and to room together. All right?" She held out the same hand that had offered comfort to Granny Hope.

Connie took it. "If God is willing, we'll go through training together. Angie, that's the best Christmas present you could ever give me!"

Christmas came in a minor snow flurry followed by brilliance of sky and world. Connie had decided to go to the hospital with Angie. She'd visit the two children who hadn't been able to leave the hospital for the holidays, while Angie read to Granny Hope.

"I'll drop you off," Aunt Ida offered. "Then I'll come back and help do the dishes while you do your angel-of-mercy errands." She looked at the demolished dinner table and groaned.

Mom chuckled and put a fresh apron over her pretty green Christmas dress. Her hands looked capable, gathering up fine china and silver from the gaily decorated table. "I'm just glad I have the dishwasher. You run along, and I'll have the food packaged away by the time you get back, Ida."

Angie would never forget that Christmas afternoon. Only a half-dozen patients remained in the hospital. Offices were closed, rooms mostly empty. Although other personnel remained on call, just a few nurses flitted through the halls, attempting to break the long, silent day between family visits.

Granny Hope sat up in bed waiting, arms crossed, grim lips in a straight line, but her face relaxed when Angie appeared in the doorway. "About time you got here." Her sharp eyes noticed Angie's dress. "No uniform. That's pretty—I can see bright red. Used to be my favorite color."

Suddenly Angie knew what to do. Before the visit she'd begged God to direct her. Now she dropped to a nearby chair. "Granny, tell me about the way it used to be." The Bible lay in her lap.

Granny's face lit up the way the Christmas candles had flamed when touched with a match. "I remember when . . ." and she was off into the past. For a long time Angie just listened, enthralled. Granny's experiences were thrilling, but even more so was seeing the crabby, lifeless person transformed into a beautiful, glowing lady.

Granny stopped. "That's enough of me. If you like, and have time"—wistfulness colored every word—"Sometime I'll tell you some more. Now, read." One bony finger pointed at the Bible. "I remember my mother used to read to me when I was small."

Angie's heartbeat quickened, and she turned to the Christmas story. She read it through, didn't hesitate, then turned to the fourteenth chapter of John. "'Let not your heart be troubled . . .'" The beautiful words sounded clearly in the quiet room. She didn't lift her head until she finished the chapter, then she said, "Granny, Jesus loves you— and so do I." She bent forward, kissed the lined brow, and slipped from the room.

A choking sound stopped her, and she quickly

glanced back in, then stood transfixed. Granny's feeble hands had captured the Bible Angie had forgotten in her hurry to get away and drawn it close to her breast.

9

Angie ripped open the envelope with eager hands. Her last letter from Dave had been a Christmas card, almost a month before. She hastily scanned it, then rushed to the door, not even stopping for a coat. "Connie!" she yelled, running across the street. "Guess what! Dave and his family are coming back!"

"I know." Connie's blue eyes somberly stared at her. "Our lease is up at the end of the school year."

Angie came back to earth with a thud. She'd been so excited over her news she hadn't stopped to think what it meant to the Gregorys. "I'm sorry. I just didn't remember . . . " She felt powerless to remove the hurt from Connie's face.

"It's all right. I got a letter too." Connie slowly drew a thick envelope from her pocket. "Angie, I have to make a big decision. Dad and Mom are definitely being transferred, but if I want to, I can stay and finish out the year here." Her smile tore at Angie's heart. "At least I know they'll be safe!"

Although Angie had suspected how deeply Connie was concerned for her parents, this new glimpse into that depth unnerved her. "Wh-what will you do?"

"I'll have to look at both sides, then pray." Connie ticked things off on her fingers. "Aunt Ida will be horribly disappointed if I go, and she really knocked herself out for me: giving up her apartment, renting this house, and all. I was just elected class secretary for second semester and appointed chairman of our new youth outreach program. Then there's Teen Aides."

"Don't forget me." Angie meant it for a joke, but couldn't hide the little tremble of her mouth.

"As if I ever could!" Some of the worry left Connie's face, and she looked happier. "If nothing else neat had happened since I came to Indian

River except finding a Jeff, I'd still feel it had been one great semester."

Angie jumped up before Connie could see how her words had affected her. "I have to get home. Studying." She paused and leaned against the polished wood door. "When do you have to decide?"

The shadow dimmed Connie's eyes again. "Soon."

It also dimmed Angie's ability to concentrate. She finally threw her pencil down in exasperation. "How can I concentrate on Oregon in the 1880s when my whole life is one big battle in the 1980s?" She lapsed into a state of numbness broken only by memory of Connie's one-word sentence—*soon.*

As if that weren't bad enough, other things began to pile up. One night she awakened to the sound of meowing. She leaped from bed, half asleep. Had Mandrake returned? Opening her window, she called softly, but nothing answered except the heavy drum of rain on the roof. Angie tiptoed past Mom's door, checked every other room. Nothing. She must have dreamed it. Yet it had been so real! It seemed she lay awake for hours, hearing nothing but pounding rain. When she finally did sleep, it was to dream of Mandrake, meowing piteously, crying for her.

Angie's mood was grayer than the still-rainy morning that greeted her the next day. "At least it's Tuesday," she comforted herself during home ec. Mom had taught her cooking years ago, and her mind roamed freely while her fingers skillfully worked bread dough into cloverleaf rolls. Granny Hope would be waiting for her, Angie knew. The old lady still had a sharp tongue, but since Angie had been either coming in early for her Teen Aide shift or staying late and reading to her, much of her quarrelsomeness had fled. She had returned Angie's Bible with the comment "I'd forgotten that Book was interesting. Might as well read it as anything."

Angie hid her surprise and smiled. Leave it to Granny Hope to go down fighting! Yet as time passed, sometimes with Angie running in between Tuesdays to spend a little time with her, she could sense that Granny Hope was gradually learning the message of salvation. Perhaps she was even close to accepting Jesus. Angie never pushed, even when she absolutely itched to make Granny respond. She just kept reading scriptures. She'd grown aware how much those scriptures were helping her as well as Granny. Connie had pointed out several that comforted; others she ran across. Or was she led to them? In spite of her own troubles about Mandrake and about Connie's leaving, an uneasy peace began to settle in her heart. She remembered her feeling at the banquet, clinging fiercely to the specialness she'd felt then and daily asking Jesus to keep her close.

Connie and Angie sloshed to the hospital after school, huddling under a king-sized umbrella that dripped streams from its edges. Shedding their boots and coats in the entryway, they carefully smoothed down the bright uniforms that did so much to bring sunshine even on dark days. Connie headed toward the office area for her assignment, and Angie automatically turned toward Granny Hope's room. The door was closed. Strange. She opened it, stepped in with a smile, and turned into a statue on the spotless tile floor.

The room stood empty.

Angie's wild gaze fixed on the two beds, neat white sheets turned back over soft green blankets; on the open closet door without a trace of Granny's clothing; on the nightstand where Granny kept her glasses. The bareness appalled her. Where was Granny? Had she—*died?*

Part of Angie's mind scoffed at the idea, telling her to walk to the nurses' station and find out where Granny had been moved. The stronger part rooted her to the floor. Memories she thought she'd banished rose to accuse her. Dad. Dave. Connie. Mandrake. Had it happened again? Granny had been improving, she knew that. What if the fact Angie had spent so much time with her had brought bad luck, and she had relapsed?

"No, oh, no!" Angie cried, feeling the blood drain from her head. She cast one more terrified glance around the impersonal room that told no secrets; then she came to life and headed toward the nurses' station. Even in her agitation she remembered Mrs. Harper's strict "Never run, even in an emergency! You'll scare the patients. Walk swiftly." Angie's knees felt rubbery, but she managed to reach the nurses' station. It was empty. What was this, a conspiracy to keep her dangling in misery?

"Need something, Angie?" a familiar voice asked.

"Mom!" Angie whirled. "What—when—where's Granny Hope?" Her breath was shallow, and she had to concentrate to keep from gasping.

"She was released today," Mom said. "Her son came for her."

"Released!" Angie caught Mom's arm and shook it. "Are you sure?"

"Of course I'm sure, honey." Mom's direct gaze pinned Angie to the floor. "What's wrong? I filled out the papers myself."

"I didn't know." Angie gulped, still hanging on to Mom. "I thought—" The terror of those moments in the silent room washed through her. From a far distance she heard Mom order, "Put your head down quickly, Angie!" She obeyed, and a few seconds later was able to stand straight again.

Mom's strong grip held her safe. Regret filled Mom's eyes. "I'm terribly sorry, Angie. I didn't dream you didn't know. It was all unexpected. Her son called and wanted to know if he could take her. Seems he's just bought a larger house, and he and his wife want Granny with them. The doctor was ready to release her a few days ago, but she had no real place to go. This worked out perfectly."

Her voice ran like water, bathing Angie in its comfort. She hugged Angie hard. "Granny Hope is much, much better. Her diabetes is under control, and she'll have her family around her to care for her."

Still distraught, Angie buried her face in Mom's shoulder. "I was so afraid—I thought—"

"It's all right." Mom cut her off before Angie could blurt out the return of her fears. "Now cheer up, will you? There are things to be done in this hospital." Her smile had never been more beautiful, and Angie didn't have the heart to tell her how close to panic she'd been. Somehow she managed to get herself together and finish her shift, but deep inside a little voice reminded, *This has to stop. You can't go on like a scared jackrabbit for the rest of your life.*

Angie didn't even tell Connie what had happened. Connie had been so proud of how Angie was handling things that Angie couldn't disillusion her. But that night she came out of bed in a single leap when she heard a familiar "Meow." Again she searched. Again she found nothing. And when she got back to bed, she had made up her mind. The next day was another teacher in-service day. She was going to search every corner, shrub, and tree for blocks around, and settle that Mandrake wasn't there and in trouble.

Her quest yielded nothing except knowledge she'd done everything she could. Even the dusty half-attic had no more to offer than old trunks of things Mom didn't want to discard. Mom's wedding dress she hoped Angie would wear one day. Great-grandma Trescott's button shoes. Crumbling pages of old letters, and the picture of Aunt Martha, who'd lived all those years before. Angie carried the faded photograph closer to the light. It was actually a reproduction of a sketch someone had made of a small, laughing woman whose resemblance to Angie was unmistakable. Same pointed face, expression in eyes, smile.

Angie sighed. How had she felt, being charged with the crime of being a "witch"? Angie knew from the story handed down it had been started by a jealous girl who disliked Martha for marrying the man she wanted. Angie also knew the severity of punishment for those accused unless they proved themselves innocent. But Aunt Martha had been a staunch Christian who faced the magistrate fearlessly, testifying with truth born of innocence of any wrongdoing. After careful examination she had been cleared, and she lived out a happy useful life, tending sick among the early people and growing loved by them.

Angie's eyes widened. Why, she was a nurse— I mean, *like* a nurse, even though she never had formal training. The thought sent shivers of anticipation through her. *Just like I'm going to be.* She rocked back on her heels. *Connie says we'll be instruments of healing.* Doubt clouded her joy. Could she overcome her own fears and feel herself an instrument, one God could use in helping others?

She sighed, replaced the things in the old trunk, and gave the crowded attic one more glance. Then she shivered. It was cold up here. Even in winter Mom left a window open a crack so moisture wouldn't gather in their well-insulated house, and the air chilled her. She groped to the window, noting how dusty it was. As soon as spring came, they'd tackle all the windows inside and out again and set them to gleaming. "I can hardly wait," she whispered. "The snow was neat and everlasting rain may make things green, but I'm getting tired of it."

There were no plaintive cat cries that night. Nor the next. But the third afternoon, Angie walked in the house, and her mouth dropped open.

A sleek, well-fed, obviously cared-for black cat sat on the hearth washing his face with a velvety paw.

"Mandrake?" it came out in a whisper. The cat leisurely crossed the room, rubbed against her ankle, and meowed in a tone Angie would have recognized at the North Pole.

She dropped her books and hugged him. "You came back! But where were you?" She held him off and surveyed him carefully. "Someone's been taking care of you, that's for sure. Your collar's gone, but otherwise you look the same." She herded him to the kitchen, fed him, and never let him out of sight the entire evening!

"I wonder if we'll ever know what happened to him, or where he was all that time," she said to Connie the next day. *Or why he went away and came back*, she added silently.

"Who knows? I'm sure there's a logical explanation." Connie's mouth curved up in a grin. "Remember when you thought you'd jinxed him?"

"Yeah. Pretty silly, huh." It felt good to laugh over the whole thing, even though Angie still felt a little twinge inside. She sobered. There was something she had to tell Connie. "Remember when you said I should go talk with Pastor Jennings?"

"Uh-huh. Did you?"

Angie took a deep breath. Held it. "Not yet, but I'm thinking about it. There are times when it all seems like a bad dream, but other times it's still too real, and I don't like seeing myself that way."

"I know he'd be glad to see you," Connie told her. "By the way, did Lance say anything about the special fellowship service?"

Angie looked up in surprise. "How come you're changing the subject?"

Connie's eyes looked lavender from the reflection of her bedspread. "Because the decision has to come from you, not from me." Before Angie could feel hurt, she added, "Just the same as my decision about going or staying has to be mine, not ours." She sighed. "It's kind of sad, isn't it? We've shared so much, but there's part of life everyone has to figure out on her own." She giggled unexpectedly. "I bet even Mutt and Jeff had to go it alone part of the time."

Angie thought of Connie's evaluation of their lives while she followed instructions on her next Teen Aide shift. For that Tuesday only she was the only Aide on duty. Connie had a touch of flu and wasn't allowed near the hospital. The others had their own shifts. Somehow the corridors seemed empty, even with nurses and ambulatory patients about. How would she survive if Connie went away for good? She tried to ignore the empty feeling in the region of her stomach. She was probably just hungry. Not long until supper.

There was no supper for Angie that night. Screaming sirens halted her halfway down the corridor. She about-faced and started back in the long, easy lope she'd learned to use in covering ground without alarming patients.

Mom overtook her, face pale. "It's a bad one. Multiple car accident in the gorge. Don't know how many they're bringing in." She looked at Angie sharply. "Can you handle it, or shall I send you home? There won't be time to care for you if you get squeamish."

"Will I be needed?"

"Desperately."

"I'll handle it." But Angie's teeth sank into her

lower lip until she tasted the sickish taste of blood.

It was the beginning of a nightmare. Angie was sent to call out every available nurse and doctor in the area. She was barely aware of their arriving, becoming part of the team sorting the critically hurt from those with minor injuries. Number after number she dialed, giving her message in crisp tones. "Emergency at Indian River Hospital. Come immediately." She had difficulty tracing one doctor, but stubbornly refused to give up. She located him at a restaurant in a nearby town. They needed every person who could possibly come.

She finished her calls, forced herself to step back into the hall, now piled with people and gurneys. What should she do next?

"Aide, tell Ida Gregory she's needed in surgery," a passing RN ordered. Angie found Aunt Ida separating a terrified child from his injured mother's arms. "I can do that," she whispered. "They want you in surgery."

"Thanks, Angie."

Angie turned to the child. "Hey, is all that noise coming out of *you?*" Her direct approach halted him in midstream, and she took advantage of the temporary silence. "Your mother needs to get her arm fixed. How about coming with me?" She could see his mouth begin to open again. His fingers clutched the mother's sleeve. "I could sure use a good helper. I'm going to see if I can keep the children in the lobby quiet. S'pose you see if you can show them how brave a boy can be. Some of them are so scared that they're getting in the way, but a smart boy like you sure can show them!" She gently disentangled his sweaty fingers, glad for the look of interest in his eyes.

"Go with her, Tim," the overstrained mother told him. "I'll come as soon as I can." She leaned limply into a chair.

Angie talked all the way to the lobby, and by the time they arrived, Tim was able to go to one of the other crying children and say, "Hey, all that noise comin' from *you?*"

Hours passed. No one thought of leaving. Two people were sent on to Portland, several others treated and released. Angie heard enough scraps of conversation to learn how the accident occurred. Fog and suddenly dropping temperatures had combined to make the Columbia Gorge an icy trap. A truck slid, cars braked, skidded, and a total of 12 vehicles were involved. No deaths, although a few were critically hurt. Thank God Indian River had a hospital! It could have been a different story if those people had faced the extra miles into Portland. Pride rushed through Angie, and she tucked a blanket from the linen closet over three children asleep on a sofa in the lobby.

"You were invaluable tonight," Mom said when they finally were sent home. In her rumpled uniform and with tired eyes, she didn't resemble the crisp nurse who had begun her shift hours earlier. "Just keeping those children amused and quiet was close to a miracle. It also meant another nurse free to do more critical duties. I'm proud of you, Angie."

Her mind kept time with the words when she stumbled to bed, too tired to even shower. No self-analysis or worrying over being a jinx tonight, she thought wryly. Her eyes popped open at the thought. Was that the key? Her overworked brain refused to grasp it, but somehow Angie knew she had hold of something terribly important, and as soon as she could, she'd discuss it with Pastor Jennings. Comfort hovered like a great protecting cover, and Angie dropped into deep, dreamless sleep.

10

Angie looked across the desk at Pastor Jennings, smiling at her with warm welcome written all over him. Why had her feet slowed when she drew near the church? Every trace of nervousness vanished, and she smiled back.

"Now, Angie," he leaned forward encouragingly. "What's it all about?"

"It's kind of hard to explain." Angie shifted her glance to the stream of light pouring in through a window. Doubts again. Maybe she shouldn't have come. It would sound strange if she said out loud what her problem was. She could feel Pastor Jennings just waiting. Not pressuring even with being there but giving her time to tell things in her own way.

Angie cleared her throat. "I guess it started when my father showed me the picture of Aunt Martha." She sketched in who Aunt Martha was and what had happened in her life. "I really do look like her, and Dad nicknamed me Jinx. He never knew how much it bothered me." She bit her lip. "He always said I was his good-luck jinx, and I never told him about the funny feeling I had every time he called me Jinx."

Pastor Jennings didn't say anything, but smiled at her again. For a moment Angie thought she saw a resemblance to her father. Maybe in the way his eyes crinkled when he smiled and how his face lit up. It made everything easier. She told him about the plane crash, how her friend Dave fell, her own resolutions to never be close to people again for fear she might bring them bad luck.

"And then Connie came." Pastor Jennings' face settled into compassionate lines.

"Yes. There was no resisting her. Besides, she carried her little Testament all the time and was so strong I knew nothing could get to her." Angie swallowed and studied her fingers clasped in her lap. At least they weren't clutching each other. "I had a pretty bad time when she was rushed to the hospital for appendicitis. Things settled down after that. We became Teen Aides, and gradually I could accept the love of Jesus I used to know when I was smaller. Then I challenged Connie to a sled race, and she took a terrible spill. My cat, Mandrake, disappeared. A little lady I read to at the hospital was gone when I arrived one afternoon, and it terrified me." Angie felt again the relentless despair of that moment.

"It was then I decided I had to come see you. I couldn't go on and on feeling I was a jinx! You can't know how awful it's been being afraid to have friends." Angie turned away, then back to give him a weak grin. "Put into words, it sounds pretty conceited, doesn't it, thinking I could be responsible for everything that happened in my world!"

"We all are affected with 'I' disease at one time or another," he told her. "Yet somehow you don't seem as concerned about it as I would imagine after hearing your story."

"A bunch of neat things have happened. Through Connie's faith I've begun to trust Jesus more. Mandrake came back. And"—she dug in her shoulderbag purse—"listen to this:

"Dear Angie,

"I thought you'd like to know how happy I am in my new home with my son and his family. His married daughter lives nearby, and my granddaughter Cathy runs over every few days to see me. She even reads to me from the Bible. This will probably surprise you a lot, the way I acted when you suggested it. I was afraid

to let myself hope you'd come and read more than once. I suppose it was silly, but I'd been disappointed with people so many times, I was afraid."

Angie broke off. "Isn't that weird? Here I was afraid I'd hurt her, and all *she* was afraid of was that I wouldn't keep coming!" She went on.

"Anyway, you were right. I've learned Jesus loves me, and if I don't have anyone else in the world, I can still have a friend. I've asked Him to be my friend, to forgive all my years of bitterness, and I know He has done that. If it hadn't been for you, maybe I would still be empty inside and a porcupine outside.

"Come see me sometime. It isn't far, and spring will be here soon. And Angie, thank you for persisting and offering love to a crotchety old woman who now deserves the name

"Granny Hope"

Angie knew her eyes were shining as much as her pastor's when she refolded the letter and put it away.

"That's a beautiful letter and one I hope you will treasure," Pastor Jennings said quietly. "Is that the reason you seem much more relaxed than you were when you first came to Indian River?"

Angie shook her head. "Not really, although I'll keep it forever. I guess what really helped was finding myself in the middle of the emergency at the hospital. After I did all I could to be useful, then went home to bed, I realized I hadn't once thought about myself and my problems. I knew I'd found the key, but I didn't understand it." She felt her breath coming in quick little puffs. "Is that what

God's been trying to get through to me all this time? That if I'm doing my best, trying to help others, I don't have to worry about *me* so much?"

A smile lurked in Pastor Jennings' eyes. "What do you think?"

"I don't know." Angie looked at him, her face troubled. "Everything hasn't been solved. Am I going to still feel I'm a jinx if Connie goes away? Or if I never solve the 'mystery of Mandrake,' as Mom calls his disappearance? I've prayed a lot and asked to be forgiven for doubting." She sighed. "I can honestly say it isn't God or Jesus I doubt, it's *me.*" She peered anxiously across the shining desk. "I've read all the 'fear not' verses, and I even thought I had this settled until that day Granny was gone and I was afraid she had died and that just maybe I was involved." There! It was out, her worst fears. She waited for his response, tightly gripping her chair arms.

"It's natural to get funny ideas about our-selves," Pastor Jennings tilted his chair back a bit, and a faraway look crept into his eyes. "All the time I was growing up, I thought I was ugly."

"But you aren't!" Angie could hardly believe it. "Why, you're—" she paused and could feel hot color pour into her face. She couldn't very well say "cool," or "neat," or some other trite word.

"Exactly." He laughed. "But it didn't do any good for people to tell me so. I was convinced I was ugly and nothing could change that." A gleam in his eyes mingled with a little shiver, and Angie knew he was remembering how painful it had been.

"That's just like me," she said breathlessly. "How did it change for you?"

"About the same way you're discovering yourself. I studied and prayed and tried to witness to my friends. It didn't happen overnight, but one day I woke up to the fact that I hadn't thought about being ugly for weeks. I looked in the mirror, and while the boy looking back at me was no star, he *was* pleasant, with a wide smile and bright eyes."

All the breath went out of Angie. "I'll bet you felt great."

"I did. All the time I'd been fighting phantoms that didn't exist—except in my own mind." His voice dropped and became more intent. "Your problem was harder, Angie, because of many things that actually did happen, although you certainly had no part in causing them."

The two sat in silence. Angie chewed on a fingernail, then, ashamed, hid her hand in her lap. "Why do bad things have to happen to Christians?" she cried, knowing that underneath all her suffering lay that single question. "Why did Dad have to die? Why did Dave and Connie have accidents? And why did I have to think I was a jinx?"

"I'm glad you used past tense, Angie." Pastor Jennings reached for his worn Bible and turned to a page. "We have our explanation right here in Matthew 5:45: 'He maketh his sun to rise on the evil and on the good, and sendeth rain on the just and on the unjust.' While God can suspend natural law, He doesn't always do it. Paul, in 1 Corinthians 1:23, tells us 'we see through a glass, darkly.' We cannot always understand God's reasoning, especially when it is in direct opposition to our own! But when we know God as a friend, we learn that He can and does bring good out of sorrow." He gently closed the Bible. "If we'll let Him, God helps us grow through our trials." He paused, leaned forward. "Angie, can you see any good that has come from your believing you were a jinx?"

Angie started to shout, "No!" She stopped, closed her eyes, and let the past months dance across her mind. Summer, autumn, winter, spring—each with new problems, new fears. *Good* from the despair she'd felt, the feeling of being torn apart? Again she started to say No. Gradually the pictures faded from her memory, replaced with new ones. Laughing with Connie. Feeling close to Jesus at the banquet. Reading the Bible to Granny and knowing that the age-old promises were for her, too. Last of all, she saw the image of a girl determined to stick it out in a crisis, praying for strength, giving all she had.

She slowly opened her eyes. Pastor Jennings sat bathed in light from the window, light that surrounded her too. Spring light. Newness of life, hope.

"Yes." Her voice was husky with deep emotion. "Yes, good has come. As long as I live I'll never be impatient with other people's fears, even though they seem ridiculous. I know what it's like. I've also learned God has given me something to use for others, my caring." She hesitated and pleated a fold of her jacket. "It's just that—every time I've thought it was over, something else happened."

"Life has a habit of doing that to us," Pastor Jennings mused as Angie stood up. "That's when the scriptures we've learned and the prayers we know have been answered come back and reassure us that God has brought us this far: He won't dump us now."

His words rang in Angie's heart giving her new courage and joy during the next few days of school. Connie never asked what she and the pastor had discussed. She did comment, "Glad you're more 'Jeffish' now," grinning her lopsided grin that always brought a matching smile to Angie's lips.

Connie also had a theory about the mystery of Mandrake. "I just bet someone picked him up when he was outside. Maybe someone who'd lost a cat of his own or who wanted a cat like him. He was obviously with someone who took good care of him and was a real cat lover."

"So how'd he come back?" Angie demanded.

Connie raised one eyebrow. "Elementary, my dear Angie. Good ol' Mandrake watched for an opportunity, and used one of his supposed nine lives to escape the clutches of the cat-napper."

"That's terrible!" Angie doubled up laughing at the suggestion.

"Do you have a better scenario in mind?" Connie stood with her hands on her hips. "I like things neatly tied up in packages, not left dangling."

Angie laughed. "So do I, in books. I hate those 'and-so-no-one-will-ever-know-if-they-lived-happily-ever-after' endings! But in real life, we don't always *get* to know." She pushed her bangs back from her face. "Wow, it's sure getting warm, isn't it?"

"Yes." Connie scuffed her Nikes along the sidewalk, kicking a pebble, finding it, and kicking it again. "By the way. . ." Her voice sounded deliberately casual. Too casual. Angie felt a flicker of warning, then Connie said, "I'm not going to stay until the end of the year."

They walked a full block before Angie could control her own voice and ask, "When did you decide?"

"During last period." Connie turned and faced Angie. "I don't want to go. I'd rather stay here and go all the way through high school, being part of this town. But the more I've thought about it, the more I've known what I had to do. Today during study time in lit I listed everything I could think of in favor of Indian River. I listed all the disadvantages of leaving now." Her voice dropped to a whisper. "Then I wrote the advantage of going. There was only one."

Angie couldn't get a word through her clogged throat.

"I wrote, 'I feel my parents need me and God wants me with them right now.'" Tears sparkled in Connie's eyes. "There was no arguing with it."

So it was all to do over. The loneliness. Facing again the loss of someone she cared for. Maybe not forever, but at least for a while. Angie felt numb, as if some giant hand had squeezed her heart.

"Don't look like that, Angie!" Connie pleaded. "There is a good side. Aunt Ida is writing to my folks and asking them to consider Indian River or at least this general area after Dad retires this summer. There's absolutely no guarantee, but there's the chance." Her crooked smile lightened the atmosphere. "I guess it's another of life's 'who-knows-if-it-will-happen' endings you hate. Me too! But I have to go to them now." She paused, picked up a rock, and studied it carefully.

"When will you go?" Angie asked.

"Monday," Connie said, and the friends walked home in silence. When they got to their homes, they simply nodded to each other. Angie's heart filled her throat. She couldn't speak. As she walked up her driveway the thought came that she'd be walking home alone for a long time. *Of course,* her thoughts jumped ahead, *Dave is coming back.* Maybe then Dave would walk her from the bus stop.

"So what?" she asked Mandrake fiercely. "When Connie leaves, half of me goes, too." She leaned against the kitchen counter, watched Mandrake sniff his food, then settle down to supper. When the numbness wore off, there would be pain. Would her terrible fear also return?

The weekend passed. And then, unbelievably, Connie was gone. Brave, beautiful Connie, clutching the flowers and candy given her, standing on the train platform, waving. Angie broke away from the crowd of students who watched the train round a bend and disappear. Connie would catch a plane from Portland that afternoon. She hadn't wanted anyone, even Angie, to go with her. Angie understood. It was one of the "me-not-we" times that life demanded, and Connie had to go alone.

Never alone. Angie remembered her own goodbyes with Connie long before they reached the station. "Remember," Connie had said. "It's Jesus plus one, even if Mutt and Jeff are torn apart."

"You sound like a wedding ceremony," Angie told her, trying to keep it light.

"Why not? In a hundred years, more or less, it

won't make any difference." Tears sprang to her eyes. "It does now, though. Don't forget our vow about nursing school."

"I won't."

Angie didn't. In the days following Connie's departure she clung to the thought. Maybe Connie's family would move to Indian River. If not, she'd keep in touch with her, and someday they'd make their dream come true. Meanwhile, she felt as if she stood at a crossroads. Lance and Tom did all they could to help her. So did others in the church youth group and at school, and Angie found that her old fear hadn't come back, just a terrible, aching loneliness.

"I used to wonder how people who'd been married and lost their husband or wife could ever remarry," she told Mom one spring evening when Mom was off duty and they'd had dinner on the patio. Spring flowers rioted all over the yard: red, pink, and white rhododendrons, tulips; daffodils; and even a few lilacs. "I think I understand now. It's to fill the lonesome spots."

"That's not all," Mom told her. "There are many kinds of love. No love replaces another, just becomes an additional one."

"Would you ever remarry?" Angie asked softly. She stared at Mom's profile, clear-cut against the padded lounge chair.

"Not unless I knew God had provided a Christian man with whom I could create a happy home and life." Mom rested her head against the back of the chair. "If I did someday, would you feel I was disloyal to Dad?"

"N-no. I might have, before Connie left. Not

now." Angie squirmed, wondering if her faltering sentences expressed what she felt. "There's this new girl at school. Her name's Peggy, and she's small and thin, and all big dark eyes with a mop of reddish hair. She's not real pretty until she smiles. No one had paid any particular attention to her until Tom brought her to youth group last week."

She sighed. "It was pretty hard for me to accept," she confessed. "I know Tom really liked Connie. Then I realized life has to go on. Peggy won't take Connie's place with Tom or with me although she's neat, and I like her."

She fell silent, studying the gently waving cottonwoods in their new green spring coats.

Mom didn't try to respond, and Angie was glad. After a long moment she said, "Mom, I have to make a choice. I can either sit around and pray and wait for Connie to come back, or try to make new friends. Maybe Peggy." She hated the quiver in her voice.

"I keep remembering what Pastor Jennings said about life having a habit of throwing something else at us once we get rid of one thing! And Connie facing forward toward a new land but hanging onto her 'Jesus-plus-one-is-a-majority' belief."

Her throat felt tight. She watched a robin cock his head to one side, listen, then dig his beak into the ground. A chattering bluejay drifted from a tall tree to the filled birdbath and proceeded to tell them off as he bathed.

Mom got up from her chair, dropped one hand to Angie's shoulder, and said, "You've learned something at 15 that many people never learn, Angie. I'm so glad." She drew in a ragged breath, and her eyes filled with tears. "After your father died, I had a terrible time wondering if I *could* go on. He'd been the greatest strength in my life, next to God."

"Were you scared?" Angie reached up to her mother's hand.

"Horribly. I didn't see how I could make it. I knew I had to for my own sake as well as yours. It didn't happen overnight. There are still times I miss him desperately. Yet God has given the gift of time to help in the healing process." Her fingers tightened on Angie's. After a moment she said, "I'm going in. Coming?"

"Not quite yet." Angie felt Mom release her hand and stroke her hair, then heard her quick steps and the slide of the patio door. Why hadn't she been aware how Mom suffered? Maybe not when Dad first died (she had only been 12), but in the months and years since.

"I was too tied up with my own fears," Angie admitted to herself. "I was so scared and angry and hurt that I never even realized it."

In a quick flash the thought she'd had earlier returned with greater force than before. "The key, really, is serving others. Mom made lifestyle changes, hid her own trouble, and concentrated on giving me a good home filled with love. She depended on God. But I was so busy wallowing in my own fears that I didn't give God a chance to help me.

"Well—" she set her chin and glanced at the darkening garden. "No more scared jackrabbit, Lord. From now on, You and I are a winning team." Angie turned her back on the darkness and stepped into her warm, lighted home.